MW00614292

A Journey to Hope

*A Yellow Raincoat
and Other Memories*

2013

A Yellow Raincoat

and Other Memories

A Journey to Hope

∾ *David A. Berresford* ∾

THE WOOSTER BOOK COMPANY
Wooster • Ohio
2008

The Wooster Book Company
where minds and imaginations meet

A YELLOW RAINCOAT AND OTHER MEMORIES

Scripture taken from the HOLY BIBLE, NEW INTERNATIONAL VERSION®.
Copyright © 1973, 1978, 1984 by IBS-STL Global (International Bible Society).
All rights reserved throughout the world. Used by permission of IBS-STL Global.
NEW INTERNATIONAL VERSION® and NIV® are registered trademarks of
IBS-STL Global (International Bible Society).

*The author can be reached at **www.ajourneytohope.net***

ISBN: 978-1-59098-332-4

JACKET DESIGN BY JEFFREY HENTOSZ

∞ This book is printed on acid-free paper comprising at least 50% post-consumer recycled fiber.

Dedication

for my lovely wife and inspiration, DEE,
and our wonderful children who are always there for us

Table of Contents

A JOURNEY TO HOPE

*A Yellow Raincoat
and Other Memories*

Introduction

Life is a journey. It is a journey filled with joy and pain, promise and despair, adventure and boredom. Each of us concurrently travels alone and in the company of others. We travel alone because each of us has a unique course. We travel in concert and conflict with others because we are affected by and affect the lives of everyone we contact.

My journey has taken me through the world of public education as a teacher and elementary school principal and my journey has taken me through the world of church ministry. It is a journey where I have traveled from childhood poverty to opportunity. Most significantly it has been a journey to hope.

It is my hope that as you read *A Yellow Raincoat and Other Memories* you will reflect on your journey—not only where you have been but where you are going. It is my prayer that your journey is a journey to hope, knowing that our hope is found in the person of God's Son, our Lord, Jesus Christ.

All that I have written has really happened and it is shared with little embellishment. Some of the names have been changed for obvious reasons but all of the individuals are real characters from my life.

—*David Berresford*

A Great New Recipe for Potato Salad

Sister Mary and Sweet William had approximately eight teeth between them. Their propensity for rubbing snuff and chewing tobacco highlighted this feature of this septuagenarian brother and sister duo. Neither Mary nor William had ever been married, although William got his nickname "Sweet" from the fact that a widow woman from down the road had a crush on him for some time.

I first met Mary and William in their rural Kentucky home when I was visiting a young preacher friend of mine who had a weekend ministry in the area. John took me to their home for dinner one Sunday afternoon. We parked on what may be called a road in front of the house. There was an unnecessary gate blocking the path in the front yard. As there was no fence to accompany it, its purpose was questionable. The path differed little from the rest of the yard and the evidence of chickens was noticeable even without the feathers. One stepped gingerly when approaching the porch. The house itself was of unpainted clapboard siding and the slate roof seemed to lean precariously.

The two siblings greeted us warmly when we entered the home. The kitchen had a wood cook stove, which added to the oppressively hot environment. Unwashed dishes were stacked everywhere. On a shelf next to the stove were three buckets of water. I found out shortly that one was for Sister Mary, one was for Sweet William, and one was for visitors to drink from. Unfortunately, there was only one ladle. I also found out later that the restroom facilities were located behind the house along the same path we had just traveled. That it was a two-seater was of little consolation.

Dinner was of humble fare, being nominally palatable. The dishes we used were comparatively clean. Having been taught the necessity of being gracious, I ate a small portion of what was available. I was doing just fine until Mary brought out her finest culinary delight. It appeared to be a pie. With a broad grin that emphasized her dental needs, Mary divided the pie into four pieces, four very large pieces, four extremely large pieces. Each of the diners received one-fourth of what I found out later was called a "chess pie" by Mary. Having eaten modestly during the main and only previous course, I felt that I would be able to handle this more than generous dessert.

Have you ever put a bite of food into your mouth and truly wondered what direction it should travel? Do you know how rich pecan pie can be? If you have ever eaten a piece of pecan pie that was really rich, as in sickeningly sweet, magnify that experience by ten. There I sat with a piece of this pie in my mouth. There was no way I could return it to its place of origin and I had no idea how I was going to swallow it. All the while Sister Mary is grinning and munching on her piece of pie and repeating, "Really good, huh? Mmmmmm, good pie."

Finally, I swallowed. It was then that I became concerned with this piece of pie, along with the rest of the meal, returning to the plate, table, and general vicinity of the kitchen. Mary continued to look at me with an encouraging smile and waiting for an expression of gratitude. I am sure my face was turning green, but I responded in the only way possible.

"Really good. Mmmmmm, good pie." Yes, I know. That wasn't exactly the truth but what could I have said? "This is the most disgusting thing I've ever tasted in my life!"

Mary was easily fooled or else I was pretty good at hiding my true feelings. "Eat up, boy."

And I did. An entire quarter of what can generously be called a pie. I did make it out of the kitchen and back to the car without becoming too sick. As John and I proceeded to leave, Sister Mary and Sweet William repeatedly invited us back for another meal. For some reason I never had an opportunity to return.

But compared to Linda Moseley, Sister Mary was another Martha Stewart. The church I was attending was having a big revival meeting, back when evangelical churches had big revival meetings. Now, an ole time revival meetin' needs a big-time preacher, a pulpit-poundin', shoutin', take-no-prisoners man of the Lord. The gathering also required plenty of rousing gospel music and heart-rending songs. Perhaps, most of all, a good revival required plenty of fine food and fellowship.

Various churches met this need for food and fellowship in a variety of ways. Some churches had dinners at the church building. Others, of a more stoic nature, sent the preacher and the host minister out to dinner at a local restaurant. But many churches had their members open up their homes so the preachers could enjoy their hospitality around the table.

Here is where the Moseleys come in. A sign-up sheet was posted in the church foyer. Members could put their name and a convenient date for an auspicious visit. Sure enough, Linda Moseley signed up for a meal after the evening preaching. The local minister and most of the congregation were aware of the fact that Mrs. Moseley was neither a fastidious housekeeper nor a great cook. However, they did not know the whole story.

And me, I was invited to go along.

The preacher, host minister, and I arrived at the home in a timely fashion after the evening services. It was a beautiful October evening with the scent of autumn in the air; that is, until you went into the house. One was aware of the presence of dogs, cats, and small children with unchanged diapers without visual acuity.

We were ushered into the living room while we waited for the evening repast to be served. The only seat that was available to me was a ragged overstuffed chair. I could only image the wildlife that probably inhabited it. I sat on the very edge of the chair and kept my eyes open for a possible attack. While observing my surroundings, I happened to glance into the kitchen only to notice that one of the family cats had lodged itself in front of an enormous bowl of potato salad. I can still hear the "ntp, ntp" sound of that cat lapping at part of our dinner.

"Time to eat." Why don't you just stand me against a wall and ask me if I want a blindfold or not? We headed to the table. The good news was that I could get out of that chair. The bad news was I had to sit in another one and attempt to eat. The preacher and the host minister sat across from me. Various members of the family interspersed themselves between us. Family members began to pile on the grub. I placed small portions on my plate knowing that I would need plenty of room to continually move the food from side to side appearing as though I were actually eating.

And the potato salad … Having seen who had previously enjoyed it, I chose to not even put it on my plate. And the potato salad … The exact same bowl of potato salad that Mrs. Moseley had taken to the Sunday School picnic the previous July. I learned two things about potato salad that evening. First of all, cats like potato salad. Secondly, it doesn't freeze well.

While I vigorously moved food about my plate and tried to focus on conversation, the action was fast and furious across from me. The host minister put a large portion of food on the preacher's plate. "Have some more, Joe."

Not to be outdone, Preacher Joe put an even larger portion on the host minister's plate and retorted, "Here, you have some more, Rob." This went on for at least fifteen minutes with each one trying to surpass the other's juvenile behavior. This behavior led to a stomach situation later that evening in the yard of the church parsonage.

What I remember most about that evening, though, was the milk. I felt that instant coffee made with boiling water would be safe. Spoon in instant coffee, pour in boiling water, reach for milk. As my hand reached for the cream pitcher, I noticed that the milk was not white as one would expect, but was pink in color. I looked about and didn't see a container of Strawberry Quick. Mr. Moseley, noticing my expression, explained, "We get our milk from the farmer down the road and he milked that cow till she bled."

OK. Having spent many years working on a dairy farm, I am well aware of a bovine malady called mastitis and its effect on milk. What's wrong with drinking your coffee black?

My wife, Dee, tells me that I am somewhat neurotic about food. I don't see it. I'm just cautious. Besides that, it's always nice to have people around that you can look down on. I am sure that everyone can relate to the advantage of feeling better about yourself because you think you are superior to someone else.

Well, let me polish my phylacteries! Is it possible that I am sounding just a bit Pharisaical? In reality, Sister Mary, Sweet William, and the Moseley family are just as good as I am. In fact, in many ways, they are better. How many of us give sparingly out of our abundance, and when we do give, we prefer to give to our kind of people? These two families opened their homes to me. They gave their best for me. They were generous, kind, and thoughtful. I believe they are the kind of people that Jesus would have had dinner with.

When I honestly assess my worth, my righteousness is of no account. When I compare myself to my Lord, I have no ability to stand on my own merit. I stand and have my being only because of His grace and mercy. May I be as gracious to all the Sister Marys, Sweet Williams, and Moseleys as He is to me.

Ebenezer Scrooge Sold Out

*E*benezer Scrooge sold out. He was doing just fine until he received those visits from the three apparitions who put the squeeze on him. He was a hard-working, thrifty fellow who had high expectations of himself and those around him. The next thing you know, he gets scared witless and is celebrating Christmas more than anyone else.

Now I'm not opposed to Christmas if you want to celebrate it. I celebrate it dragging and kicking all the way to the mall. My wife believes that I make pre-spirit visited Ebenezer look like a soft touch. I've not always felt this way about the Christmas season.

As a small child my parents did the best they could with the money they had to make Christmas a special day. I can remember the terrible time I had going to sleep on Christmas Eve and how I would wake up and be ready to go at 4:00 A.M. and 5:00 A.M. and 6:00 A.M., not realizing that my mom and dad had been up half the night making preparations. And the joy of rushing to the tree to open presents once the go ahead was given! One sad thing that was always in the back of my mind was the fact that Christmas would be another year away before I could experience this joy again.

Even during this time of childhood bliss, Christmas had a downside. During one Christmas break, a neighbor child told me that when we returned to school we were supposed to take one of our presents with us. Since he was a big kid and I was only a second grader I heeded his advice. That first day back, proud as any child could be, I took a large model car to school with me. My dad was especially happy to have been able to afford this gift for me. Into the classroom I went to be greeted by my teacher, Miss Handslapper. "What do you have there, young man?" I thought it was rather obvious but having been called, "young man," I knew I was in trouble and had better not be smart. I was clueless as to what I had done wrong.

"It's a car I got for Christmas."

"I can see that. And why do you suppose you should bring it to school?"

I explained in my best second grade rationale why I brought the car to school and was positive that such an explanation would put me back in her good graces. She explained that since she had not told us to bring anything to school, I could set my car, my very best Christmas present, on the table in the back of the room. She went on to tell the whole class that they could bring a Christmas present to school with them when they returned after lunch. At that time all the children would be permitted to play with those presents and share them with others if they desired. That is, all of the children except me. I was to return to school without any additional gifts and the one I brought was to sit by itself on the table while I sat by myself at my desk. What the Ghost of Christmas Future could do with that woman!

Third grade was even worse. When I was a child it was common to have a Christmas tree in the school. Our school building was a large, two-story affair with a landing on the stairway that was as large as some classrooms. It was here that a monstrous, heavily decorated tree was placed. The warning went out to the whole student body. "DON'T TOUCH THE TREE!"

It was during a restroom break that the criminal activity took place. We all lined up for break. Lining up was a really big deal in the 1950s. Lines were to be kept straight. Hands were to be kept to one's self. And no chattering. Chattering was one of the Biggies and no one wanted to be caught doing one of the Biggies.

My third grade room was located on the second floor and the restrooms were on the first. The line proceeded down the stairs toward the landing. And there, one class in front of ours, a fourth-grade boy touched the tree. Actually he did more than touch the tree—he pulled on the sacred monument. Nothing happened. No bells or whistles. No alarming siren. Nothing. Finally, students in my class began to pass by Old Tannenbaum. Suddenly, there I was, right beside it. I could smell its pine fragrance. I could see my reflection in its glorious bulbs. I could reach out and actually touch it with my own hands. And I did. A voice from above shouted, "HE TOUCHED THE TREE!" And another and another. It was a symphony of accusing voices and pointing fingers. And then THE voice, the voice of old Miss Broomstick, "You, Mr. Berresford, come here right now."

I walked slowly up the steps. All eyes were on the condemned. The whispers sounded like a muffled roar. After the lecture, the punishment was handed out. From that day forth until the beginning of Christmas break, I was to go to the restroom by way of the fire escape. No individual of my corrupted nature could be trusted to again pass by the honored conifer.

The fire escape trip only lasted for a week. My reputation followed me for years. By the middle of fourth grade my family had moved to Ohio. I hope it had nothing to do with my infamous deed. One summer we made a visit to my grandparents' home back in West Virginia. I was in junior high. I was standing in Grandpa's back yard when a voice from the alley behind the house shouted, "Hey! You're the kid that touched the Christmas tree." The young teen that yelled was serious. He was always serious. He later went on to become a teacher and then the assistant principal in charge of discipline at the school where I began my teaching career. I never told him that I was the tree toucher of his youth. I wanted to keep my job and get good classroom evaluations.

In spite of these setbacks, I continued with a Tiny Tim spirit. When my children were young, the joy of Christmas morn was rekindled. I loved the Christmas programs, especially when they were participants. The seasonal songs filled my heart. Family gatherings of food and fellowship warmed my soul.

But now, I'm a cynic. It's not that I haven't tried to get the Christmas spirit. I'll listen to the songs. I check out the decorations. I go to the family gatherings. I buy presents and love giving them, but I still have a rotten attitude about the whole thing and end up getting very sarcastic.

To start with, I have to share my adult children with several other families. Between in-laws and out-laws, it's a major logistical challenge to get everybody together at the same time. When we can get together most of us are exhausted from all of our other get-togethers. Christmas parties are another drag on the schedule and most people seem to come out of a sense of duty. Well, at least that's my motive.

And the shopping. Advertisements for shopping used to begin after Thanksgiving and that was too early in my opinion. Now, as soon as Halloween is finished, out comes all the Christmas glitz. It is amazing how many businesses survive only because of Christmas sales. I hate Christmas shopping. I actually hate any shopping, but it is especially bad at this time of the year.

And when I really think about it, this gift giving isn't too great either. Look at it this way. You spend $20.00 to buy me something I really don't want so I can spend $20.00 buying you something you don't want. Would it not be more practical if you just kept your twenty bucks and I kept my twenty bucks and we could buy something for ourselves that we each really wanted?

And now that we're talking about the giving routine, what is it with this Santa Claus issue? Here we have an old guy in a dirty red zoot suit saying, "Hey little kid, wanna sit on my lap?" As an advocate for children I have a problem with this. And to top it off, he offers them toys, free of charge, mind you, if they just come over and talk to him. I warn kids not to take gifts from strangers and they don't come any stranger than a guy who lives at the North Pole, hangs out with elves, and runs around promising free stuff.

Look at the guy. Makes these tiny reindeer fly all around the world pulling a sleigh loaded with toys. Where's PETA when you need it? And the old guy himself, the old bowl full of jelly, would do well to go on a low carb diet.

I'll be honest with you. If some individual shows up in the middle of the night in my house with a bag over his shoulder chanting, "Ho, Ho, Ho," I'm calling

9-1-1. Instead of serving him milk and cookies, which we already established that he definitely doesn't need, he is going to be serving five to ten years for breaking and entering. If you believe he's there to leave you gifts and is not robbing you blind, I have some ocean-front property in Arizona to sell you.

And the decorations. At least do me the favor of not putting them up until December 1st, and please don't wait until June to take them down. Here we have snowmen, and Santas, and the poor helpless reindeer, and there we have those goofy, fake-looking icicles. The lights are everywhere; electric lights, no less, and this with an energy shortage in the world.

Please don't misunderstand. I have spent time dreaming of a white Christmas and all the other Bing Crosby feelings that go with it. But instead of a White Christmas, I always end up with a black slush Christmas.

Maybe the real problem is my dreaming of a white Christmas instead of dreaming of a right Christmas. Now if I were dreaming of a right Christmas, I would imitate the behavior of the wise men who traveled a long distance to bring gifts to a poor family in Bethlehem. They gave out of the goodness of their hearts without any desire for a return on their generosity.

I imagine that a right Christmas would involve coming to bow down and worship a promised child who brings hope to the world even as poor shepherds did on the night of that child's birth. It would include praising the God of this universe as the angels did on that most glorious of nights.

A right Christmas would see a young mother giving birth to her first child under the most adverse conditions. It would anticipate the price the child would pay as a young man that we might have hope in Him.

I believe that the giving, the decorations, the singing, the fellowship, and all that we associate with this season, takes on a whole new meaning when looked at through the window of Bethlehem. I believe that the true Christmas spirit comes with adoration for the Spirit of Christmas.

What Policeman Behind Second Base?

My wife is an avid football fan. If you saw her on the street, her petite appearance and generally quiet demeanor would dissuade you from believing that she is a jumping up and down, screaming at the television, football fanatic. Dee knows the game and she knows the players, especially if they are Ohio State Buckeyes. Her enthusiasm for the Buckeyes even exceeds her general love of the game. When Ohio State won the national championship in 2003, I thought we were going to have to call a cardiologist.

Unfortunately, my wife's knowledge of football does not carry over to an even remote understanding of the game of baseball. Dee's only exposure to the nation's pastime was watching our grandson play T-ball. This became starkly real to me when we were given tickets to a Cleveland Indians baseball game recently. She was excited to go even though she was not sure what the experience was going to be like. Having personally been to a pro baseball game, I was happy to be at a big league stadium with all of its atmosphere. I did dread facing city traffic and parking problems, but that goes with the territory.

When we arrived at Jacobs Field the mood was electric. The Indians were having a winning season and the stands were packed. The vendors selling their products added to the fun. And the tickets we received … two box seats on the third base line. We were so close we could see the expressions on the players' faces. A couple of Coneys and colas and we were ready for the ump to shout, "Play Ball!"

It wasn't until the third inning that reality set in. After observing the first third of the game in a rather passive manner, my wife looked at me and very unpretentiously asked, "Why is there a policeman behind second base?"

"Why is there a what?"

"Why is there a policeman behind second base?" I was glad that she knew what second base was but couldn't see the policeman she was referring to.

"What policeman?" What else could I ask? Besides that, the next player was coming to bat and I *did* want to watch the game.

"The man in the policeman's uniform behind second base."

It finally dawned on me that she was referring to the umpire behind second base. There was no doubt in my mind, knowing my wife, that the next six innings would be spent answering every question she had thought of during the first three.

Dee had noticed that some of the players were separated from the rest of the team and situated along the right field side of the stadium. It never occurred to me that the location of these players would be an affront to anyone. The fact that they were kept behind a chain link fence added to her aggravation.

"Who are those guys behind the steel fence?"

"What guys?" I was starting to feel like I was in an Abbott and Costello routine and the next question would be, "Who's on first?"

"The guys behind the steel fence, over there." Dee pointed in the direction of right field.

"Oh, you mean the bullpen." I really didn't want to see the home run I missed because I was looking in the wrong direction.

"The what?"

"The bullpen." I figured that I had better take the time to explain as quickly as possible and get on with my observation of whatever inning of the game we might be in now. "The bullpen is the place where relief pitchers wait until they are needed. If the manager calls for one, he can warm up and then he comes in and takes the other pitcher's place."

I am not a master teacher for nothing. Matter settled!

"That's not fair!"

"What's not fair?" We'd gone from Abbott and Costello to Burns and Allen.

"That those guys have to sit out there away from the

rest of the team."

"They don't mind. They like it out there. Besides that, it's their job."

"Aren't they a part of the team?"

"Yes."

"Then it's still not fair." I believe that the Indians were up by four runs then, even though I couldn't remember anyone crossing home plate recently. "If they are a part of the team they should sit with the team up there," she notes, pointing at the dugout. "I'm sure it hurts their feelings." Dee was really into the self-esteem thing at the time. And trust me, I did not refer to the location of the rest of the team as the dugout since this was not a double-header and we were running out of time.

By the bottom of the eighth inning I had gone from being amused to irritated with Dee's concerns over baseball diamond etiquette. My only hope was that it couldn't get any worse. There was at least an inning to go, maybe more if the Indians fell behind. At least I could see the finish of what was possibly a good game. Base hit to left field. Indians have a runner on first base. No outs. I was into it. Cleveland manager calls a time-out. Pinch runner goes to first. Player who got the single leaves the field to the applause of the fans. Speed on first, no outs, the cheers began to soar.

"Where did the other guy go?"

"What other guy? Let's go Tribe! LET'S GO TRIBE!!"

"The guy who hit the ball."

"They replaced him with a faster runner." "Let's go Tribe!" The count is two and one. The pinch runner is taking a bigger lead off first base.

"That's not fair!"

"What's not fair? Let's go Tribe!"

"The other guy does all the work, gets on base, and then he doesn't even get to run around the rest of the bases."

"We will never get to see anyone run around any bases if you keep this up," I mumbled to myself.

"Dear." Have you ever noticed how that word can be used with different inflection? "The manager wanted a faster man to run for the team. They do it all the time. It can help them win." I figured I'd have to watch the evening news to see who won the game I just *watched*.

"Well, does the man who hit the ball get to come back and play some more?"

Now going through my mind is a moral dilemma. Do I lie and tell her, "Oh sure, he is getting something to drink and will be right back." Or, do I tell her the truth and pay the price for my honesty? Call me foolish but I opted for the truth. "No Dee, the man who was replaced cannot come back in the game."

"I told you it wasn't fair."

"Are you ready to go home?"

"The game's not over, is it?"

"It has been for me for some time now."

Dee and I proceeded to the nearest exit. As soon as the field was out of sight, I could hear the crowd cheer. Another missed home run. It didn't take us too long to find our car. The anticipated trip home would take about forty-five minutes. That we beat the crowd was one good thing about leaving a little early. Jump on I-90 to I-71 south, no big deal. Being a real guy, I have a built-in compass, a true sense of direction on the highway or in the woods. Who needs directions? We got here didn't we? Forty-five minutes later, we were somewhere on the east side of Cleveland on 480, or 77, or …

"Shouldn't we stop and ask for directions?"

"No, dear. I know how to get home." What an offense to my manly pride!

Ninety minutes later I finally swallowed that manly pride and asked for directions. I really didn't want to spend the night in Erie, Pennsylvania.

About four hours after we left Jacobs Field, we made it home. Needless to say, Dee and I have not been to a baseball game since our odyssey to Cleveland.

Upon reflection, I'm sure that Dee really felt out of place at a professional baseball game. She was excited about the possibilities but her limited frame of reference kept her from what should have been a great experience. She was confused and became frustrated at her lack of understanding. She probably believed that she was the only one out of 50,000 fans that was totally clueless.

Have you ever been there? You could see and hear the cheering crowd but you really didn't fit in with them. They seemed to know something you didn't. You were, at least in your mind, an outsider.

Unfortunately, I think that this is an experience that too many people have when they enter a twenty-first century church gathering. We, as fans of the church, understand all the nuances of the game. We have our reserved seat tickets. We know when to stand and when to sit. When communion is shared or offering collected, we know the drill. We know how to act when a pinch preacher is sent into the game. We have, and are, our favorite players. The team's songs are familiar on our lips and sometimes stir a memory of bygone victories.

What about those who are not familiar with who we are and what we are about? When they show up on the church doorstep, are they coming with great anticipation of what may be? Have they heard that our team has something great to offer? But, is their curiosity and anticipation turned to confusion and frustration because we assume they know, "What meaneth these things?" Do we judge them because they are not wearing the right uniform or question what we do? Or worst of all, do we simply ignore them?

Now I'm not suggesting that you give up your seats, only that you consider sharing them. It's not necessary for you to get new uniforms. Just remember that it is perfectly all right for new fans to dress a little differently.

And you definitely do not need to abandon all of your traditions. Traditions can be great things if they are not held to at the expense of the truth. Simply be aware of the fact that not everyone understands or believes in what you practice.

I am suggesting that we be prepared at all times to give reason for the hope that we have and to be sensitive to all we meet (see I Peter 3:15). We all may be surprised at how full the stadium becomes and how many new victories the team wins. After all, we have the best coach and manager in the universe.

The Dearly Departed

I buried a woman.

And I'm not talking about one of the numerous funerals that I have participated in, even though they have provided some very interesting experiences for me. Some of these funerals have been extremely sad. Probably the most difficult for me are those of children and young adults. On many occasions, in the process of trying to give strength and consolation to the family, I became so emotional it was hard for me to speak.

My first funeral was for a lady I had visited many times before her death. I was close to part of the immediate family and was very conscious of their grief. The funeral service proceeded as well as could be expected. Background music was played as the family sat waiting for the eulogy. The chapel was full. I waited in the corridor outside the funeral director's office. I could hear the sobbing over the music. It hurt me to hear people I cared about in so much pain. Finally the director sent me in. The casket was behind me and to my left. I set my Bible and notes down on the lectern before I ever looked up.

I took a deep breath, said another quiet prayer for strength and for the right words, raised my eyes, and began the message. I know that I did not speak for more than twenty-five minutes but it seemed much longer. After the message, I went to the front row and said something personal to each member of the family.

After the casket was closed, and this was the first time I had ever seen a casket being closed, I walked in my appointed spot, accompanying the pall bearers. The casket was placed in the hearse. I rode to the grave site with the funeral director. He made jokes while I tried to remember how I was to consign this body to the earth from which it came. Upon our arrival, we walked the casket to the grave. The final words were said. The final prayer offered.

The family was preparing to leave when a commotion came from the parking area. Jumping out of their car was one of the departed woman's daughters and her husband having supposedly just arrived from Arizona. The fact that she had spent the morning at a local beauty parlor was too obvious. Then the wailing began. As she ran through the graveyard to the casket, her recently arranged coiffure started to come undone. Freshly applied makeup was smearing all over the woman's face. Hysterically, she was crying, "I want to see my mother, I want to see Mom!"

Since Mom was already bolted in by the funeral director, we had a dilemma. Before that day, I had never seen a previously closed casket opened. The director opened the casket. To his chagrin, Mom was somewhat disheveled. The recent arrival was howling uncontrollably. The rest of the family, who had attended the service and had reached a point of some closure, now began to sob and cry all over again. I stood silently in the background. To this day, I have no idea as to what I should have or could have said at that time.

Other funerals have had elements of humor that point to a more poignant truth. Prior to one funeral service I officiated for a man whose family I did not know personally, a rather inebriated middle aged man approached me.

"Are you sa preesher?"

"Yes. I will be sharing the message today. Is there something special you wanted me to say?"

"Preesher, jus go eeshy on me."

"What do you mean, go easy on you?" I honestly had no idea where this fellow was coming from. I did know where he had just been, though.

"Jus go eeshy on me. I can't teg it."

Finally, I got it. This fellow did not want me preaching repentance or talking too much about death or anything like that. It was well outside of his comfort zone.

I was not unkind but perhaps a bit offended. "I'll be

sharing the message from the scriptures that I brought today."

"Oh no preesher. Not thaat. Ohhh, I can't teg it."

I was shocked when this man started crying, but in his condition I could offer him little help. I remember him standing in the back of the chapel throughout the service actually trembling.

But, like I said, I buried a woman.

I received the telephone call on a hot summer day. A trustee of a cemetery that I helped care for needed someone to dig a grave. Mowing grass and straightening tombstones is one thing, but digging a grave is something else.

"I don't have a backhoe and that ground is all stone."

"No problem. The funeral director only needs a hole dug approximately twelve inches square and two feet deep."

Let's see, a hole twelve inches square and two feet deep. "And who are we digging this grave for?"

"Some woman. And the undertaker wants it dug directly over her husband's grave."

"Let me get this straight. You want a hole dug on top of the grave of some guy. It's to be twelve inches square and two feet deep? And you are going to bury the guy's wife in it?"

"Right. Oh, I forgot to tell you, she's being cremated." It really would have been nice to know that at the beginning of the conversation.

"OK, I'll do it. When is the service?"

After getting the details, I headed off to the graveyard, spud bar and posthole digger in hand. I easily found the husband's gravesite, sort of guessed as to the best place to dig, and began the task. I was somewhat tentative in my labor, not wanting to disturb the old fellow and having no prior experience in grave digging.

The funeral director, preacher, and immediate family of the departed arrived sooner than I had expected. When I saw them pull into the drive, I picked up my tools and discreetly moved off into the distance and stood waiting under a tree. The preacher offered the traditional words, the family said their last good-byes, and then the director approached me. Although he did not visually size me for a casket, his presence still made me a little nervous.

"She's all yours."

"She's all mine?" There are many responses I could have given in retrospect, but that is all I could come up with then.

With a sideways smile, "She's all yours. Just put her in the hole and cover her up. She's leaning against the tombstone." With that, the preacher, funeral director, and immediate family left the graveyard.

So there we were, "Her" and me, just the two of us. And she was all mine! I approached her as cautiously as an adolescent boy on his first date. Sure enough she was in a small box leaning against the tombstone. Now what do I do? Slam dunk her into the ground, kick on a little dirt, and take off?

Instead, I got down on my knees and gently took the box holding the earthly remains of what was once a human being. I placed those remains into the earth as delicately as I could. I took my bare hands and scooped the dirt from the little pile that I had recently made and I covered her. These were the earthly remains of someone who had been an infant in her mother's arms and a small child in school. She may have been the little girl who always raised her hand with the correct response or the child who was too shy to answer her teacher's questions. She had been a child who ran and played and cried and laughed. Did she go to the school prom? How excited was she when the man of her dreams asked to marry her. This was a wife and a mother. She held her first-born in her arms at the hospital and undoubtedly wondered at her own child's future. She had dreams and hopes for herself and her family. Did she ever realize these dreams? She had suffered loss and had stood in the very place I now stood as her husband was consigned to the grave.

So I thought. Is this all there is? You live on earth playing a role that has been given to you. A few words are said, a few tears are shed, and that's it? You even cease to be a memory in such a short time. Life goes on, and without you. Is there not more? For those whose hope is in Christ, the answer is a resounding, "YES!" Yes there is more and better.

"When the perishable has been clothed with the imperishable, and the mortal with immortality, then the saying that is written will come true: 'Death has been swallowed up in victory. Where, O death, is your victory? Where, O death is your sting?' The sting of death is sin, and the power of sin is the law. But thanks be to God! He gives us the victory through our Lord Jesus Christ" (I Corinthians 15:54–57).

Turkey Gobbler and the Cadillac Eldorado

Thanksgiving is a great holiday. At least it is in my family. You sleep in late unless you are my wife who has to get up early and begin preparing the meal. When you finally rouse from a complete night's rest, many options are open to you. You may choose to go rabbit hunting, a great Ohio tradition, unless you are opposed to shooting Thumper. You can always watch the Macy's Thanksgiving Day Parade, or plan your football viewing strategies, or mess around in the basement or garage pretending you are working. Unless you are my wife who is still preparing the meal and setting the table.

When all of the company arrives there is a great warmth that accompanies the smell of roasting turkey, fresh pies, and other delights that my wife has been preparing all day. At last we sit around the table, say our prayer of thanksgiving, and start filling our plates, unless you are my wife who is making sure that everyone, including the grandchildren, has been served.

After a huge meal followed by a piece of pie or two and a cup of coffee, it's time to head for the living room to watch a football game and take a nap. (Turkey does have tryptophan in it.) Except for my wife who is busy cleaning up the dishes and packing away leftovers so we will be able to enjoy them for days to come. Dee makes great turkey gravy and biscuits.

Like I was saying, Thanksgiving is a great holiday: plenty of food, fellowship, and fun. OK, so I exaggerated a little bit to make a point. Please don't tell my chauvinistic friends, but I do help prepare the food and setting for the Thanksgiving festivities. So do our children and grandchildren. The point is, Thanksgiving is a matter of perspective because thanksgiving is a matter of perspective.

My perspective on Thanksgiving changed dramatic-ally shortly after a telephone call I made several years ago. The call was made to Margie and to the best of my memory had something to do with a church youth activity in which her children were participating. Margie was a single mom with three children. Her husband had abandoned her shortly after the third child was born. She was as hard working and gracious as any person I had ever met. I never heard Margie complain and she always had a smile for everyone and a helping hand for anyone who was in need. Knowing this, it was somewhat of a surprise when I rang the number to her house and heard:

"Turkey gobbler."

"Hello?"

"Turkey gobbler."

"Margie?"

"Is that you, Dave?"

"Yes. What's with the turkey gobbler routine?"

Margie went on to explain that the local radio station was giving away a free turkey if they called your home and you answered, "Turkey gobbler." I knew then that Margie didn't have the money for a Thanksgiving turkey for her family because there was no way she would have answered the telephone that way if that were not the case. I finished my conversation with her and immediately headed for the local supermarket.

I asked for and purchased the largest turkey that they had in the store, took it to Margie's house, and asked her to please not answer the telephone that way any more. Telling her that was the only thing I could think of to help her not be embarrassed by her need.

Please understand. I am not sharing this so you will think I am this super generous person. On the infamous day of "turkey gobbler," Margie gave me one of the greatest gifts I have ever received and one I will never forget. The look on her face when I handed that turkey to her still brings a tear to my eye. That expression of gratitude for a minimal effort on my part brought to life the words of Jesus, "It is more blessed to give than to receive" (Acts 20:35).

Years later I was sharing this story in a Sunday School class I was teaching. Just as I reached the crucial point of the lesson that Margie taught me, a young man in the class yelled out, "Cadillac Eldorado." Nice try Mac, but I think you missed the point. I think many people miss the point. For them Thanksgiving is little more than food, fellowship, and fun; thanksgiving is too often a casual awareness that we have been blessed in some ways.

I cannot speak for you but I have so much to be thankful for. My wife is a source of support and joy and enriches my life every day. Those children and grandchildren of ours are such a blessing, such a source of joy. We are not wealthy by American standards but our needs and wants are taken care of. And our Lord has not only provided an abundance for us in this life, He has given us the hope of everlasting life in Him.

Unfortunately, like many people, I too often lose sight of all the wonderful blessings He has given me and focus too much on the problems of this world. I worry and permit those worries to steal my joy. Paul encourages his Philippian readers to "Rejoice in the Lord always. I will say again: Rejoice! Let your gentleness be evident to all. The Lord is near. Do not be anxious about anything, but in everything, by prayer and petition, with *thanksgiving*, present your requests to God. And the peace of God, which transcends all understanding, will guard your hearts and your minds in Christ Jesus" [emphasis mine] (Philippians 4:4–7).

As a young man I worked with a preacher who spent a good deal of time trying to impress people. Every

Sunday morning for four weeks this man stood before the congregation and prayed, "Thank you Laorrd for all the vicissitudes [said quickly with the emphasis on the third syllable.] of life and we praise you for them." The context of the prayer indicated that a vicissitude was something you would eat for supper similar in use to the term "victual." I suspected that the man had no idea what the word meant, had heard it someplace, and decided using it would make him appear more intelligent than he really was. Being a curious fellow and not wanting to thank the Lord for something questionable, I checked with Mr. Webster. Finding that a vicissitude was a favorable or unfavorable event or situation that occurs by chance, or it may be a difficulty or hardship in life, I knew the man had no clue. Or did he?

Our God is in control of this universe. I do not believe that things happen by chance or fate. But on the other hand, do not even many of the difficulties we face in life temper us and make us better people as we rely on Him by faith? Cannot the ups and downs of our lives hone us to become better tools in His service? Maybe I should be as thankful for the vicissitudes as I am the victuals.

The Psalmist tells us to "Shout for joy to the Lord, all the earth. Worship the Lord with gladness; come before Him with joyful songs. Know that the Lord is God. It is He who made us, and we are His people, the sheep of His pasture. Enter His gates with thanksgiving and His courts with praise; give thanks to Him and praise His name.

For the Lord is good and His love endures forever; His faithfulness continues through all generations" (Psalm 100).

The Psalmist understood that thanksgiving was not a day but an attitude of life.

I Absolutely, Positively Hated School

I hated elementary school. I am sure that to many readers this is an unusual comment coming from a former elementary school teacher and principal. But nevertheless, I absolutely, positively, hated elementary school. There are many reasons why this may have been true. I'm sure that I wasn't always the best behaved or brightest child in the classroom. My attention surely was missing at times. But how can I account for such an overpowering negative reaction to a significant and influential part of my life?

In sharing this experience with you, I do not solicit your sympathy although a little may salve my injury. What was wrong with elementary school? I got a bum deal! Plain and simple, I was robbed. Now I'm not bitter about what happened but have found it to be a great learning opportunity for me as an adult.

I never went to kindergarten. Maybe that's the problem. Poor start. Robert Fulghum said everything he needed to know he learned in kindergarten. First grade holds little recognition in my mind. My teacher seemed to be absent without leave even when she was present in the room. On one occasion when she was on a break and we were left alone, I went to front of the class and pretended like I was the teacher. Of course I was caught. Perhaps what I learned more than anything else in first grade was not to get caught.

My second grade teacher was an old spinster who by some trick of fate was also my next door neighbor. Her claim to fame was quickness with a ruler. One must remember that one's little finger should not protrude as one writes his letters. The word 'protrude' had little meaning to this second grader but the smack with the ruler left an indelible record on my mind. To this day, to prove a point, my little finger protrudes as I make my scribbles on sheets of paper. So take that!

But third grade, that was the crème de la crème. What a teacher! There is no doubt in my mind that this woman worked nights in the theater. Her only role was chasing small children around in Oz cackling, "I'll get you my pretty." Years earlier, and she was old then, this same woman had my uncle as a student and he was probably the worst kid that ever attended this elementary. He terrorized the woman. When I found this out years later, he became my hero. Somewhere in this eccentric individual's mind, she must have thought I would serve as a payback for my uncle's behavior.

I remember many things clearly from Miss Broomstick's classroom, especially the spelling tests.

Spelling tests were a special event for this teacher and I am sure that she was preparing students for work in the Secret Service the way she administered them. Papers were torn neatly in half. Name was placed in the top right hand column along with the date. The non-writing arm was held in such a manner as to preclude any other students in the room from copying from his neighbor. As words were presented, she paced slowly up and down the aisles, insuring that honesty would prevail. At the end of the test, all students were to turn their papers upside-down. Pencils were to be placed inside the desks. Hands were to be neatly folded on top of one's desk. I am still not sure how to neatly fold hands.

Oftentimes on my test, words that were spelled correctly were marked incorrect. There was no place for discussion as to the infallible judgment of my teacher. But what's a fellow to do? I could handle it. Like I have told my children and my students, "Life sometimes isn't fair." But on one occasion, during one of these infamous spelling tests, I had what I might call "a defining moment" in my life, such as life is to a third-grader. I had finished the test. My pencil was placed inside my desk. My hands were folded on my desk. Suddenly, a voice came out of the blackness as if from under a house in Munchkin Land. Surely the woman deserved an Oscar or at least a part in *Whatever Happened to Baby Jane?*

"Cheeeeeeater!! There is a cheater!" I looked to my left and to my right. No cheaters there to my knowledge.

Behind me. No way. "Cheater, you come up to the front of the room, right now." It finally dawned on me that she was talking to me. But what brought on such wrath, such vehemence, such indignation? And there it was on my desk. A pencil. Granted, there was no point with which to write. And I had already eaten the eraser for a late morning snack. But nevertheless, a pencil had remained on the top of my desk in plain view of the honesty police.

"Bring your paper to the front of the room, cheater." I made a journey of what seemed like miles and minutes. Snatching the paper from my hand, she marked a red "F" about the size of the Washington Monument on the test. There I stood in front of my peers as she pronounced judgment for my infamous deed.

"Hold this up for all the class to see. Class, this is a cheater and this is what happens to a cheater." Miss Broomstick believed that total humiliation in front of one's peers was adequate punishment and would serve to emotionally scar a person for life. She was probably right.

This is only one of the many wonderful days that I spent in third grade. Perhaps what bothers me most as I reflect back on this time is that in spite of the way she treated me, I still tried to please her. Sometimes I wish I could have been more like my uncle, but then, he grew up to be a small-time criminal.

By fifth grade my family had moved to another school district in a bordering state. Unfortunately both states used the same mold for their teaching staffs. The good news in fifth grade was that I was among a select group of students to represent the school in a choral presentation. The bad news came about during the first group practice. The music teacher gathered all of the vocally gifted into one classroom. Anticipation was high. She stood in front of us, directing us to the first selection. I think it was after three or four notes that our director called for a halt. Something was wrong, terribly wrong. She asked for different sections to sing and leaned her highly trained ear in the direction of each group as they traversed the musical scale.

Then it was my group's turn. We were an outstanding group of young men located in the back row. I personally felt that we all sounded pretty good, especially for a grade-school choir. She didn't. Someone was noticeably off-key and would need to return to their classroom. Such musical clinkers could not, would not be permitted in our school's choral presentation. It was then that I noticed her long, pointed, bony index finger, which also served as her director's baton, rise ominously. Upon whom would this fearful appendage come to rest?

"YOU!"

"me?"

"How were you ever chosen to be a part of this group? You have no singing ability whatsoever. Return to your room at once."

The appendage tracked me as I slithered back to my classroom. There I had to provide an explanation to my fifth grade teacher as to the reason of my early return. The disgust in her reply indicated that she expected as much from me. Not only had I interrupted the choir by my presence, I had interrupted her class by my return. For some reason I have not been comfortable singing in public since the day I was drummed out of elementary choir.

My first male teacher came when I was in sixth grade. Mr. Friendly had a dislike for me for which I was much thankful in later years. Unfortunately he did have special students that he actually called his "teacher's pets." These boys, and they were always boys, had the privilege of sitting next to his desk as long as they remained in his good graces. Sometimes it is best to go unblessed by someone's favor.

Junior high was hardly better than elementary school and high school was a joke. It was the sixties. Students were unruly and unqualified teachers were pulled off the street. My whole high school experience can probably be summed up in one event. I was a senior and was in a college prep English class. The teacher was arrogant and overbearing and I had reached a point in my life where I really didn't care. One day he had called me to his desk to clarify his expectations of both my behavior and work ethic. Upon returning to my desk, in a voice loud enough to be heard at Central Office, I noted the fact that he was related to the canine species on his mother's side of the family. Well, it wasn't exactly in those words, but then again I wasn't always Christian in my behavior. What I find interesting is that his subsequent explosion had no effect on me. I had become numb to this institution called public education and the heartless, mindless people that promoted it. I had no confidence in them and less in myself.

The lessons I learned in school did not come from these individuals; it came because of them. One of the reasons I became a teacher was to make sure that every child I had, had at least one teacher who cared.

When I look back and see the whole picture, there were those teachers, those people who were exceptional and wonderful people. They were individuals who made a positive difference in my life. Mrs. Johns, thank you for helping me in fourth grade. I am sure that you saw how Miss Broomstick was and you made a difference. Thank you, Mrs. McIntosh for making me feel welcome in a new school. I cannot remember one specific lesson either of you two taught, but I do remember that you cared.

Recently, I worked with some of the greatest teachers in the world. They used the best teaching strategies available. They worked tirelessly and exemplified professionalism at the highest level. But, most of all, they cared. I would ask that anyone who works with children to first and foremost show that you care. Children may not remember what you teach them, but they will remember who you are and how you treated them.

This is not only true in the teaching field, it is true in life. People will remember little what we preached to them. They will always remember how we treated them. Throughout our lives we have had contact with those individuals who have hurt us through what they have done or failed to do. Sometimes they have been family and friends, other times they have been total strangers. They have left wounds on us.

We have also been blessed by those special people who have lifted us up by a kind word or deed. Perhaps when we were at a low point in our lives, someone came to us with hope or help. Many times this one has been a quiet supporter in the background. Many times the act is as simple as a smile.

We affect people's lives, whether we want to or not. We affect every individual we contact in some way, and how we treat them impacts on how they feel and how they act to some extent from that point on. From that perspective, we change the world each and every time we interact with another human being.

We must each ask ourselves, "How do people truly see me?" "How will they remember their relationship to me?" "Am I an encourager, a hope giver, or am I a joy stealer?" The words of Jesus give us the best direction when He says, "Do to others what you would have them do to you" (Matthew 7:12).

So Much for Anonymity

One of the issues I have wrestled with for most of my life is my temper. I have tried at times to mask it behind flowery terms like "righteous indignation," but most often it's just an expression of personal anger. My temper has been a cause of embarrassment for me on numerous occasions. At other times it has caused me physical injury.

As a young man I was an avid sports fan, especially of the local high school team.

I attended most of the football and basketball games and tried to keep my fanaticism under control. I even attended games out of state when the locals were experiencing even nominal success. During one two-year span our basketball team had a great athlete who was being touted as first team all state. This young man had the ability to carry the whole team on his shoulders. Wherever he went, he filled the gym. One such gym was out of state against a bitter rival.

The place was packed by the time I arrived at the game. I slid in between a couple of fans on the away side bleachers; ready to watch an inferior team get trounced. By the end of the first quarter, our star had two fouls on him, very questionable fouls to which our fans expressed a measure of displeasure. By the end of the half he had two more fouls that were even more suspect in their legitimacy. Our fans expressed a general discontent with the officiating crew. The physical well-being of those officials was really not in jeopardy regardless of what may have been said. Personally, I did audibly note that such observance of the game on their part was dubious and their homes were probably located in the proximity of the players on the opposing team.

Since we had superior athletes, we were positive that the game could still be won. Our star, even with four fouls was able to lead to victory. The tip off for the second half brought a roar from the crowd. Our star had tipped the ball to one of his teammates who led a fast break down the floor. Star was all by himself in the middle of the court. Not one player of either team was within fifteen feet of him. Whistle. "Foul on number 22." Who? Number 22? Our star player? "That's number five, son. You're out of the game!" With grace the young man walked to the bench and sat down.

The fans from the opposing team jeered and cheered. Our fans booed and hollered. And what did I do in the heat of the moment? I was so agitated with the injustice of the moment that I proceeded to the scorer's table, slammed down a nickel, pointed to the official who had made the call, and yelled, "Give it to him, he earned every penny of it."

Have you ever been in the process of doing something that you knew was really stupid but for some reason you couldn't stop yourself? If you have, you understand my frame of mind. I knew I had stepped over the edge the minute my hand slapped that nickel down. Do you also know how a million thoughts can go through your head in an instant?

As the nickel hit the table and I knew I shouldn't have done it, I was also aware that all of the fans were standing and there was so much noise, no one would see or hear me. Would they? Then, above the uproar of the crowd came a voice from ten rows back, a voice that could be heard above the crowd by everyone in the crowd.

"Put one down for me too, Dave?" So much for anonymity during a moment of stupidity. The voice belonged to one of the members of the congregation I attended. So much for being a good Christian witness of self control and proper priorities. I slinked out of the gym that evening. For the next several months I had the opportunity of hearing the story retold to a group of amused brethren after every church service.

There were other occasions when I had wrestled with this weakness and lost. Explaining to my doctor that my hand was broken because I hit a brick wall, twice no less, at the local YMCA because I missed a layup playing basketball was humiliating. Returning to the Y when my hand had healed was equally difficult. Nor did such an outburst on my part improve my game. Telling the podiatrist that my toe was smashed because I kicked a cow brought the house down as he assured me that my case was totally unique. Everyone in the podiatrist's office stopped by my room to check out the unique case of the cow kicker.

Probably what epitomizes these incidences most is a situation that took place on a winding back road near my home many years ago. I was driving a 1972 Buick Electra Limited with a 400 cubic inch engine with a four barrel carburetor. I was turning into a driveway that was at a difficult angle on a hillside and had to slow down almost to a stop to make the turn. Just as I turned, a fellow drove up beside me, laid on his horn and started screaming at me. He told me to do things that I thought were anatomically impossible and probably illegal in at least forty-seven states.

As he proceeded on down the highway, I felt that we needed to further our discussion. I backed out of that driveway twice as fast as I had pulled in. As soon as my car was on the road I tramped the gas peddle to the floor. Do you know what happens when you tramp the gas peddle to the floor on a 1972 Buick Electra Limited with a 400 cubic inch engine and a four barrel carburetor? Actually, nothing. It sort of sat there and warmed up. After a few seconds, it began to roll. Finally, I was after him and once that 1972 Buick Electra Limited with the 400 cubic inch engine with a four barrel carburetor began to roll, it was like a steel-hauling truck flying down a hill. Fifty miles per hour, sixty, seventy and I am gaining on him. I can see that the fellow can't handle the bends.

After one hair-raising turn, a question came to mind. What are you going to do if you catch him? That is, if you don't kill yourself first. I slowed the car down, turned around and sheepishly headed for home, hoping no one had seen my little outburst.

Before you are too hard on me, I have improved dramatically in this area of my life. During one of my job evaluations when I was a principal my superintendent commented on how calm and laid-back I was. I never seemed to get real upset about things. I shared with him that when I was younger I fought constantly with this temper issue. He asked how I was able to get it under control. Although I have not totally mastered this issue in my life, I explained that there were two reasons why I felt I had improved. First of all, many experiences that I have had have helped me to mature. Secondly, and more importantly, my faith has helped me to overcome this lack of self-control. I realized some time ago that most of the battles I fought could not be won by my own might. It is by His grace that the victory can be mine. It is His Spirit that helps to overcome and greater is He that is in me than he who is in the world (see I John 4:4).

Remember, though, that I'm not the only one with weaknesses. Everyone has faults or weaknesses.

I hate to use the word "sins." It tends to make people uncomfortable and none of us like to be uncomfortable, especially when it comes out of a confrontation with the truth. What is it that holds you back in your race of life (see Hebrews12:1)? What is it that hinders your witness and robs you of your joy? You can overcome because He has overcome the world (see John 16:33).

Additionally, we must be honest and reflective in examining our own lives. We cannot afford to play the game that my sins are the little ones and yours are the big ones. To do so is to be guilty of advising others to pull the splinter out of their eye without noticing the beam in one's own eye (see Matthew 7:4).

Paul admonishes Christians, "Brothers, if someone is caught in a sin, you who are spiritual should restore him gently. But watch yourself, or you may also be tempted. Carry each other's burdens, and in this way you will fulfill the law of Christ" (Galatians 6:1, 2).

Scrunched Up Faces and a Movie

*E*ntertainment was at a premium when I was a child. By the time I was in second grade my family had improved their financial position a bit and was fortunate to own a used black and white television that got a fuzzy picture on a good day. Saturday mornings were great fun when I was able to sit on the arm of the couch, toy guns in hand, shooting at the bad guys when I watched Roy Rogers, Hopilong Cassidy, The Lone Ranger, and The Cisco Kid. Every morning before school was Captain Kangaroo. Bosco and Ovaltine were big sellers on the commercial scene. I still remember watching the *Wizard of Oz* while eating homemade chocolate fudge with my mother. It wasn't until years later that I found out that after the opening scene everything was in color.

Since I was entertainmently-challenged, I was thrilled when the town fire department decided to show a movie at the local theater and permit all the neighborhood children to come free of charge. A free movie in a real movie theater, and a box of popcorn went with the deal, was something that made my heart skip a beat. The movie was to start at 1:00 and I had to walk several blocks from my home. I left early enough to get a great seat. I was shocked at the size of the line when I arrived. Looking up at the marquis, I saw the title of this anticipated delight, *Abbot and Costello Go to the Moon.* I walked past the ticket box, then the usher, and took my seat. The lights dimmed. The curtains opened. The silver screen began to flicker with life. And there they were, Abbot and Costello, before my captivated eyes.

I settled in my seat, eyes glued to that screen, popcorn in hand. Abbot and Costello were one of the funniest comedy teams of all time, right? I was ready to laugh. I wanted to laugh. But then, shortly into the film, came the shock. A vision of terrifying creatures appeared before me, and in a comedy no less. I covered my eyes to no avail. I knew they were still there, scaring Costello as badly as they were scaring me. I endured as long as I could endure. But I could not take it. It was too frightening and I left the theater.

Once I reached the safety of the afternoon sun and began to start home, all my fear was dispelled. I questioned both my bravery and my sanity. For what reason had I walked away from a dream come true? How badly I wished to return to that place of entertainment bliss. So I did return. I approached the outside of the theater with some hesitation. How could I reenter? I had already used my get-in-free kid opportunity. They had seen me walk in and undoubtedly had seen me flee but moments earlier.

A plan. I needed a plan. Let's see. Any kid could get in free and I had used up my big chance. But … but if I looked like another kid and fooled them I could slip in and they would never know the difference. It was starting to come together. No time for a change of clothes. Got it! I scrunched up my face to the degree that I was sure to be non-recognizable and walked through the doors of the theater avoiding all unnecessary eye contact. Now, to get past the usher. Eureka! It worked. No one had a clue as to my identity. I had fooled them all and was able to watch the remainder of the film with little concern that they would seek me out and force me to leave.

A scrunched up face can serve different purposes. It may be used to show a general discontent with life giving a "stay away from me message" to the observer. We sometimes have difficulty promoting the ideal of Christianity and the love of God because we appear so joyless in our day to day lives. How many unbelievers look at professed Christians and comment, "If his belief makes him that unhappy, I want no part of it?"

More often a scrunched up face is used as a matter of pretense, even as I used it many years ago at a movie theater. Unfortunately, all of us at some time have pretended to be something we are not. We have put on an artificial face to meet an individual purpose. It's called being a hypocrite. I understand that the origin of the word hypocrite is found in theater. Greek actors used masks to portray a certain characteristic. The audience saw the outward face of the performer and was unaware of what was beneath the mask. A good actor had the ability to change masks without the audience being aware of that change. Suddenly and subtly the actor took on a new persona.

As Christians, we are to be sincere in our persona to all those around us, not one with two faces. An individual who is sincere is without anything counterfeit in their nature. Ancient artists, in order to salvage a flawed sculpture, would use tinted wax to cover the flaw. All went well until the buyer placed the insincere piece in the sun. As soon as the heat reached it, the wax melted and the sculpture was seen for what it really was, a fraud. We may be able to hide who we are for a period of time, but when the heat of trials challenges us, we are found wanting and fraudulent.

I clearly understand that a person can be sincere and be sincerely wrong. If I believe that a stick is a rattlesnake, I will respond to my perception accordingly. I would sincerely believe I have seen a snake. I will sincerely react as though I have seen a snake. Nevertheless, the object remains a stick and I would be sincerely wrong, although not as wrong as I would be if I thought a rattlesnake were a stick.

Jesus said that God is a spirit. Those who worship Him must worship Him in spirit and truth (see John 4:24). We have been given the truth of God's Word as a standard to determine if our sincerity and our emotional expression of faith are correct or misguided. On the other hand, how many individuals are aware of the teachings of His Word and yet live a life of pretense?

For example, when I am at my secular job and I talk and act like the worldliest people there, it will make it very difficult to explain to them how Christ has made a difference in my life. They will see no difference. It will not matter that I put on a Sunday morning halo, sit in the choir, and teach a Sunday School class. My co-workers will see past the religious mask and my witness will have no positive effect.

If I am constantly angry on the highway and practice digital diplomacy with those with lesser driving skills, when I pull into the church parking lot I may hear the words, "Another hypocrite."

Our lives must sincerely reflect our love of God if we are ever going to win the world to Him. Sure, we may be able to scrunch up our faces and fool the ushers and ticket takers of the world for a period of time, but our Lord always sees beyond the mask. We should ask, "What does He see when He looks at me? Who lives behind the mask?"

Birthdays Are More than Singing Chickens

I'm just not a party animal. Anyone who knows me personally knows that if I go to any kind of party, I look for a corner to hide in. Conversations are not meant to be a group activity, but a quiet, unobtrusive exchange of ideas. One of the worst things a person could do to me is throw a surprise party on my behalf. My staff was well aware of this truth, which is why they probably did things like this to me all the time.

My birthday was treated like a national holiday in the elementary school in which I served as the principal. I have walked into my office when the walls and doors have been covered with signs and the room filled with balloons. On one occasion the staff gathered around my office door along with a singing chicken that clucked Happy Birthday. Of course a picture was taken of the chicken putting its wing around me.

The students always got into the act. The entire building would sing Happy Birthday to me at the same time and every child I spoke to on my birthday, and for a week afterwards, made a big deal out of it. I did appreciate the acts of thoughtfulness of my students and staff; I just didn't care for all of the attention.

One of the activities I did like was receiving homemade birthday cards from the children. I could read them in private and smile at their bits of wisdom and kindness. A couple of themes were reoccurring in many of the cards.

The comments on a homemade birthday card are just great. "Have very much fun. I like you." I would have had more fun without the singing chicken.

"It's your 100 birthday right. I hope I don't get in trubl [sic]." First of all, your teacher is in trouble for not doing a better job teaching spelling. And secondly, "100 birthday?" And you wanted to start having recess again someday?

"I love you." I got this all the time. Trust me, I never had a principal I could have said that about. Don't let this out, but I loved every one of the children and staff members in my building.

"You're doing a great job! You are doing such a great job that if thare's [sic] a contest you would win 1st place!" I don't think that spelling is a big issue at all. It's the purity of expression that really counts.

"You are very nice to everybody." Obviously this young lady never read my chapter on anger. "I'm glad that you protect us." That made me feel important. "Thank you for getting this job. You're a great princible [sic]." Like I said, spelling is not that important.

"Coolest principal ever."

"I wouldn't want any other prinibal [sic] besides you! Your [sic] the nicest pricibal [sic] in the world."

"You have made our school wonderful!!" When you are a child you can use as many exclamation marks as you like.

On a card shaped like a star, "You are a star principal that shines bright in our school. Thank you for making school fun." I made sure that this child received all A's on her report card.

"You are a good principal. You smell good." That's definitely better than not smelling good. "You are not mean at all." If he would have told me I didn't smell so good, his feelings concerning my meanness may have changed.

"There is no other princial [sic] as special as you."

"You're the best principal I ever had." Yes, but I was the only principal you ever had.

From another A student, "You are the best person. Your [sic] awesome. Thank you for being kind. Your [sic] the best principal. You rock. Your [sic] special as gold."

When I read these and the many other cards I received, I began to grasp what an important fellow I must be. "Greatest," "best," "good smelling," "nicest," "awesome," "special" are all words a wonderful person likes to hear.

But then there was that one card. Now keep in mind that I'm a man with a full beard. The card came from one of my third-grade boys and very clearly stated,

"Happy birthday you old hairy thing." Excuse me! Do you not know that you are speaking to Mr. Greatest, Best, Nicest, and Awesome Special Principal who just so happens to smell good as well? When I read that card I rushed straight to that child's room and called him into the hall.

"Did you write this card?" I asked in mock anger.

"Yes, sir," he contritely replied.

Then I burst out laughing, "That's one of the funniest things I ever read in my life."

The child was relieved and smiled but I doubt he ever fully understood why I thought it was so funny. You see, he actually, even if by accident, struck on a truth. No matter how many accolades an individual receives and regardless of how many wonderful deeds he performs he is not righteous in and of himself in the eyes of God. "There is no one righteous, not even one" (Romans 3:10). "For all have sinned and fall short of the glory of God" (Romans 3:23).

We are all from the same mold, perhaps some a little moldier than others, but nevertheless, we all fall short of the mark by our own merits. My third grader was right in this respect; outside of Christ, I'm just a hairy, old thing and really don't smell so good after all. But there is hope. And that hope is in a birthday. Not the birthday that marks my years on this earth, but a birthday that marks my rebirth in Christ. In Him, I become a new creation (see II Corinthians 5:17) and can be a sweet savor to the world around me.

One card I received deeply touched me. A little girl wrote, "Dear Mr. Berresford, Thank you for being a good example for all the kids in the school. Let Christians be a good example for you." I hope I taught my students as much as they taught me.

Snowmen Fall from Heaven Unassembled

*P*arents come in all packages. Most are conscientious and try very hard to do what is best for their children. Some even try too hard. Others, well, others probably should not have had children to begin with. Parenting class could help many adults, but some of the individuals who teach parenting are poor parents themselves. Many of us are critical of the parenting that we see, especially when we are in public. Few of us are critical of our own parenting skills. I am no exception.

For example, don't you just love those parents that you see in the grocery store whose kids are indulged whiners? Little Mary begins to act out. Perhaps she has asked for her fiftieth candy bar. Mom says very nicely, "No, you have had enough candy for now." Mary begins the routine, the one she has used successfully most of her young life.

"I want a candy bar."

"No, Mary, you can't have a candy bar."

Is Mary dissuaded? No way. She has played this game hundreds of times and has seldom lost.

The crying starts. Perhaps a little kicking and thrashing accompanies the well-rehearsed tears. "But Mommy, I want a candy bar."

"Mary, I'm not telling you again, no candy bar."

Yeah, right, Mom. Pretty soon little Mary is walking out of the store with more chocolate on her face to accompany her "I won again" smile.

Little Teddy is a child I met in Indiana. I was working with a congregation there for a couple of weeks and was staying with his parents. At the ripe old age of three, he already had control of the household. Dad was a public school psychologist/minister and Mom was an expert on everything and therefore did not need any form of gainful employment.

On one occasion, Dad was listening to classical music while sitting in his easy chair looking intelligent and important. Mom was in the kitchen working on some health food concoction, which was actually inedible. I was sitting in a state of total boredom until Teddy decided he did not like the sound of the classical music on the record player. To make his point, something he was exceptional at, he began raking the arm of the record player back and forth creating a large needle gouge in the record.

At that instant, Mom calmly asked, "Dear, (obviously not speaking to me) should we not restrict Teddy from playing with the record player?" (He did not look like he was playing to me. He seemed pretty serious about the whole business.)

Dad's response was equally calm. "It's OK, honey (hopefully not speaking to me), that's why we bought a used phonograph so we would not have to worry about it."

Teddy's behavior was equally refined in public settings. After church services one evening, we went to an ice cream store and were all served sundaes. Teddy was not to be left out of the festivities and likewise received an adult portion. Do you have any idea how many square feet of space in a store can be covered with ice cream from one adult-sized ice cream sundae? I did after that experience. Again, Mom and Dad did not see any problem with their son causing a great deal of extra work for the staff in that establishment. Nor did they see any negative impact on their Christian witness to the employees.

Fortunately, Teddy and I reached a working relationship soon after we met. His mother and father had asked me to watch him while they went to the store. He was to be given a bottle (Yes, I did say he was three years old) and put in his crib for his afternoon nap. One of young Teddy's games was to throw the bottle out of the crib and determine the number of times an adult would pick it up and give it back too him. I'm sure his parents did not need to take aerobics classes with this a part of the daily routine. So there we were, Teddy and the Bear (That's me.). Teddy smiled, threw the bottle onto the floor, and waited. I picked it up and handed it to him. I then told him that if he threw it out again, the bottle would stay on the floor. Teddy was not a believer. After Teddy threw the bottle out the second time, I just smiled and went about my work. Teddy became a believer. A few whimpers, a little fuss, and the game was over. I wonder if Teddy (hopefully Ted by now) is a believer now or if he is still playing games with people.

Raising children should be a relatively uncomplicated task. If parents follow a prescribed pattern, they are sure to get favorable results in return. If the results are unfavorable it can be attributed to the fact that the parents did not use the correct child rearing strategies. Perhaps you have heard this advice before. Maybe you even heard it from me because I used to give it all the time. That is, all the time before I had my own children. I have to admit that prior to having my own children I was a consummate expert on the subject. Since they came into my life, my knowledge on the subject has declined steadily and rapidly.

It's not because I did not read the proper books on the subject. Nor is it because I did not seek out advice. And I will guarantee that no father could love his children any more than I did and do. I'm the father who went into my children's bedrooms in the middle of the night and woke them up to make sure they were OK. And worry—I probably can worry about the safety and well-being of mine better than anyone I know. And I prayed and continue to pray everyday for them, but nevertheless, I worry. I spent as much time as I could with them individually and collectively while they were still at home and I tried to capture and enjoy every moment knowing how quickly they would grow up.

But still, I made so many mistakes it's a wonder that they have survived at all. Granted, I had no experience raising children before I had children. When they got older it dawned on me that I had as much experience raising a child as they had at being a child. We were sort of learning together. But the mistakes I made …

For example, when my daughter was about six years old and my older son was four, they were constantly picking at each other. Pick, pick, pick. It was driving me crazy, as you will soon realize. I had had it. Every parent in the world knows what I mean when I say, "I had had it!" I was sitting in the living room trying to read and relax and these two children started at it again. Please remember that, with no exaggeration, these two are really very kind-hearted individuals. The gremlins had just gotten them.

"All right you two. Out in the yard. NOW!" I used my very best Dad voice. And out into the yard they went with me following close behind. They had no idea that I had been reading a good deal on child psychology and was about to effectively apply my knowledge on them.

"Rachel, you stand here." And she stood facing her brother.

"Jonathan, you stand here." He was already where I wanted him to be but I needed to set the stage for what was about to happen. They never saw this one coming. It was Dad at his educated, expert best. The day I couldn't outsmart a six year old and a four year old ...

"Now I want to see hitting, kicking, scratching, and biting. I want you two to go at it right now. Get it all out of your system." I had them right where I wanted them. They looked at me incredulously.

Now, I would use this strategy to drive the point home and give them a lesson that would take care of the problem for the rest of their lives. I was on a roll. "OK Rachel, hit your brother. I want you to hit him real hard. If you want to fight with him, then do it right."

"But I don't want to hit him." Am I good or what? One down.

"Jonathan, I want you to hit your sister. Come on. Hit her hard." I could hardly keep from grinning. Just a little more and the victory was mine.

"Come on, Jonathan. You want to fight. Hit her."

Smack. This boy doubled up his fist and hit his sister as hard as he could in the mouth. She started to cry and he just stood there. Now as I share this, please do not report me to Children's Services. Remember too that we are outside the statute of limitations.

"All right you two. Back in the house. Now." I had to maintain some semblance of control. Back in the house they trotted. I followed close behind knowing that no book would get me out of this one.

I returned to my chair in the living room and

pretended to read while trying to decide how I could apologize when I heard a conversation in the hallway.

"I'm sorry, Rachel. I didn't want to hit you. He made me do it."

"I know, Jonathan. It's OK."

They went on to play together. I was relegated to "he," the ogre that made his little boy hit his sister in the mouth.

My children did not need psycho babble but they did need tough love and direction. All children do.

My wife and I were recently walking through an arts and crafts festival and noticed a placard that stated, "Snowmen Fall from Heaven Unassembled." The saying and the little pictures that accompanied it amused me. The saying also brought to mind my struggles trying to be a great father.

When we are blessed with children in our lives they do not arrive fully assembled. They are incomplete emotionally and socially and their physical development has a long way to go. And they do not come with a complete list of instructions so we will know what to do as parents each step of the way. It is our responsibility, with God's help and the assurances that we receive from His Word, to cultivate their physical, emotional, intellectual, and social maturation. It is also our responsibility to guide them in their spiritual growth.

The Gospel writer, Luke, tells us that when Jesus returned from Jerusalem at the age of twelve with Mary and Joseph that He was obedient to them and that "[He] grew in wisdom and stature, and in favor with God and men" (Luke 2:52). What a marvelous outline for homes, schools, and churches as we look at what we should be doing to meet the needs of children! We could even look at this outline as instructions for proper assembling.

As a parent, teacher, and principal, I would recommend to every parent several things to accompany the admonition of Luke. I have learned many things too late and I am sure that I have learned too little about raising children but I do know some never-fail strategies.

First of all, capture every moment. I can't tell you the number of times I fussed because of something my children did or did not do when they were small. Somehow, when they became young adults, handprints on the wall weren't so bad after all. And their friends coming over weren't such an interference to my schedule and those visits should have happened more often. Don't overlook the little things they do and as much as possible take time to listen to all of their stories and concerns. Hug them more often and you can never tell them too many times that you love them.

Practice good discipline but always with love and the desire to help them become more God-like in their character. Remember that discipline is to change behavior, not to vent your personal frustration. Also remember that discipline is not just correction, it is also instruction. Take every opportunity to teach them, "What meaneth these things." And discipline has to be consistent. Many children spend a childhood in confusion because parental expectations change constantly.

Instill values so they know what is right and wrong and model the behavior you wish them to emulate. Attributes like honor, goodness, and kindness must be cultivated with children and witnessed by them in others. And praise your children when they do well. Give them specific directive praise as an encouragement.

Don't be afraid to admit that you are wrong. It's good for them to know that yes, you do make mistakes and yes, you are honest enough to admit it. And don't be afraid to laugh at yourself. You and your children will both feel better when you do.

And parents, please do not live vicariously through your children. I dealt with one father who was a mediocre football player on a small town high school team. His son, a third-grader at the time, was entirely "too artsy" for his personal taste and he wanted his boy to be Joe Athlete so he could cheer for him from the stands and say, "That's my boy." To Dad, this boy was in sad shape. For this dad it would have been bad enough if his son were interested in soccer, which he thought was for girls and Europeans. But it was worse. Of all things, this child, now brace yourself, this child wanted to be in the band when he was in high school.

Your son may never be the star football player or your daughter the best volleyball player or homecoming queen. They may not be class valedictorian. That's OK. Each snowflake is an individual. Each has its own beauty. Honor that.

And most of all, train up your child in the way of the Lord and when he is old he will not depart from it (see Proverb 22:6).

Courage in Small Packages

All of us face fears throughout our lives. Sometimes it takes the courage of a child to dispel those fears and give us hope.

Let me introduce you to Little Sport. I met Sport when I was doing inner city work in Baltimore, Maryland, in the mid-1960s. A group of students from the college I was attending was working in the city in conjunction with a local church. Every Saturday we went to selected children's homes and then escorted them to the church where we presented lessons. After the lessons, we returned the children to their homes. Due to the nature of the neighborhood, we always traveled in twos. Because we were helping neighborhood children, the people who lived there always treated us with respect.

As I recall the neighborhood, I can clearly recollect the tenement houses set side by side, block after block. The first three floors of these multi-story buildings were generally reserved for family dwellings. In many of the buildings anything above the third floor served as a business area for the oldest profession. The smell of cheap perfume and the lighting selections were a dead give away.

One of the first homes this naïve seventeen-year-old entered on a warm fall day had the stench of aging garbage. The hallway was so narrow that two people could not pass each other. My partner and I, both new to the program, were there to pick up two children who had been participating in the education program for several months. After climbing up two flights of stairs that had been borrowed from a Dickens novel, we reached our destination. An individual I found to be beyond adequate description answered a knock on the door. To this day, I do not know if it was a mother or father, an older brother or sister. We entered the apartment on one level and followed the individual on a narrow path through two trash-filled rooms and exited the dwelling at another level. As soon as we walked into the hallway, it became entirely clear as to the source of our olfactory dilemma. There it lay, stiff and fly-covered. The comments of the child caregiver accompanied our observation.

"Oh, don't mind that. One of my cats died the other day and I've not had a chance to throw it out yet." I did not dare ask where "out" was.

A few weeks later the children from this household became heroes of mine. After picking them up, we went to another home and had to wait in the living room while one of the children finished getting ready for class. As I was standing there, one was cautious about sitting down; I noticed that the walls and floor were almost covered with my least favorite creatures. Some people are terrified of spiders. Others deplore mice and rats. Some quail at the thought of a snake. For me, the most despicable creature on earth is a cockroach. Now I mean no personal offense to cockroaches or their human advocates, but for me personally, the only good roach is a dead roach. As I guarded my pant legs and stayed clear of walls and furniture, my youthful companions took serious action. With their bare fingers they began plucking roaches from the wall and squashing them in the myriad of ashtrays that were in the room. The smack-splat sound was music to my ears, as I knew it meant another roach had met its demise.

In contrast to these children were a couple of boys who lived in the same neighborhood but were always clean and well-dressed. The apartment they lived in was immaculate. I could not understand in this area of poverty how these two could appear so well-off financially. It was only when I found out that their twenty-two year old sister made a great deal of money working as a call girl that I understood. Her questionable vocation provided her the funds she needed to care for her younger siblings.

The most interesting child I met during my time in Baltimore was the aforementioned Little Sport. We stopped at Sport's home to escort his older brother and sister to the church building. Sport had never before attended the lessons even though he was of an age to do so. I knocked on the door and was invited in with a yell from across an inside room. Upon entry, the first thing I noticed was Dad sleeping on a bed in the living room recovering from an overnight bout with alcohol. In the kitchen were Mom and some friends having a morning bottle of beer and meeting the needs of their nicotine habits. After a quick hello to those who were awake, I noticed the little fellow. He was tied up, hand and foot with a rope, and lying on the floor. Seeing him in this condition, I started to untie the helpless little tyke.

His siblings warned me, "Whatever you do, don't let him loose!"

The injustice of it all! How could parents permit a brother and sister to tie this little guy? How could these children have the nerve to warn me not to free him of his bondage?

I bent over the incarcerated youngster and with perfect indignation loosed the bonds of his captivity. Before I could straighten up, he grabbed me around my neck with both his arms and wrapped his legs around my waist. It was a death grip.

His brother yelled, "I warned you," and he had.

I finally freed myself from the child I had freed. His mother was more than happy to let him attend the classes for the remainder of the day and quickly gave her smiling permission. Sport insisted that he ride piggyback to the church building, which was several blocks away. My adult companion agreed to provide this mode of transportation for him. Sport wrapped his legs around by friend's waist and his arms around the guy's neck. Like I said before, Sport was capable of a death grip when he took hold of you. We traveled no more than fifty feet when Sport let go with his arms and fell backwards laughing hysterically. It was all we could do to catch him before his head hit the concrete. The remainder of the trip consisted of trying to keep Sport's head away from the sidewalk and supervise five other children at the same time.

Fortunately, Little Sport was not one of my students once we reached the church. He quickly took control of his classroom by crawling under a table all the while threatening the other students in his group. He also threatened to bite the teacher and urinate on her at the same time. Admittedly, it would have been interesting to see if that were possible.

On the way home, I took charge of Mr. Sport. "You WILL walk young man, and you WILL stay with the group." And he did walk with the group, at least until we came to the first of several neighborhood taverns. At that point Sport broke from the pack and ran full speed into the tavern and to the far end of the bar. I was elected to go in after him. Although it was a bright, sunny day, this building was dark and smelled of stale cigarettes and liquor. When I caught up with the fugitive, he was talking to another child who I had not seen when I first came through the doors. The boy was Sport's twelve-year-old brother and he was shining shoes making a few dimes the only way he could. Rarely after that first day was Little Sport available to go with us again as he never seemed to be at home.

I have no idea what happened to Little Sport, the two neatly dressed brothers, or my heroes, the cockroach killers. I do know that I often think about them and wonder what happened to them. They were children who were survivors in a very rough environment. I hope that they continue to survive and that they were able to step beyond the limitations of that environment.

The children I worked with more recently are generally from entirely different kinds of homes with different types of problems and issues in their lives. Their problems can be just as real and their courage just as great.

For example, Daniel was a fourth grader in the school in which I was the principal. He was one of the brightest children in the building and excelled in all academic areas. He had the most charismatic smile I had ever seen and did a great imitation of Oliver Twist complete with the British accent. When he was in second grade he came up to me at the end of one school day. Even though it was my birthday, it was one of those days you would love to forget. Everything that could go wrong did go wrong. Daniel had something to share with me and I was in no mood for sharing anything but my lousy disposition.

"Mr. B., I've got something for you."

"And what is that, Daniel," I replied with a very artificial smile.

"It's your birthday hug." At that point Daniel gave me a huge hug that came straight from his heart. Both my smile and my restrained tears were from my heart.

Daniel had that effect on people. He could walk into a room and the whole place was brighter because he was there. Perhaps that doesn't seem too unusual or special until you know a little more about Daniel. He was one of the smallest children in the building, including the kindergarten children. You see, Daniel has a life-threatening disease. It is a disease that impacts every aspect of his life. No one knows better than Daniel that his life cannot be, will not be, like almost every other child he knows.

Daniel probably had the right to be angry and depressed. Perhaps he should have expected others to always try to lift his spirits. But whether he was at school, in the hospital, or at home, Daniel was too busy bringing joy to the lives of others to feel sorry for himself. Daniel's courageous spirit gave me the encouragement that I often needed. This small package of a boy with the giant heart makes the words, "Let the little children come to me, and do not hinder them, for the kingdom of heaven belongs to such as these" (Matthew 19:14), take on a very personal meaning. Heaven must be full of little Daniels.

Strike One – You're Out

All labor strikes are traumatic experiences, to say the least, but teachers' strikes are to me especially ugly. Not from the standpoint that they are as violent as many industrial strikes but because of the manner in which they affect children. There are no winners and many losers. When I was a fifth-grade teacher I was involved in a very bitter six weeks teachers' strike.

For three years prior to the strike, animosity had been building between the teachers and the administration. The district superintendent was Old Snake Tongue, a nickname the teachers gave him since they thought he wouldn't tell the truth even when it was in his own best interests. He started on a rampage almost immediately after he had signed the previous negotiated agreement. He felt that the teachers had gotten the best of him. Every time there was a disagreement between the superintendent and the teachers, the contract would be pulled out. The president of the union would point to the specific item in the contract and Snake would say, "I know that's what it says, but that's not what I meant."

Several issues ended up before an arbitrator who invariably ruled in favor of the union.

When time for negotiations came up, Snake decided to take a new approach. "This is what I am offering, take it or leave it." As even the most ardent anti-union person could not accept such an unfair proposal, the teachers voted to leave it. The vote was 100% in favor of going on strike. No one on either side of the fence could have foreseen the price that would be paid by everyone as a result of the superintendent's proposal and its rejection.

I have to be honest and say that the first few days of a strike can be rather exciting. The state union representative, Sleaze (my personal name for him), came to a big meeting giving everybody the assurance that the strike wouldn't last long, that the administration would buckle, and that all the parents would support their children's teachers. He should have also offered us some cheap ocean-front property in Arizona. He also admonished us to abide by the law.

Our strike was different as we were trying to set a precedent in Ohio. We were going to teach the first half of the day, leave the school buildings, and picket the second half of the day. I just love being a test case. It rates right up there with being a guinea pig in a laboratory. That first day, I taught as normally as I could, removed all of my personal items, and asked my students to behave when they brought in the "substitute" teachers. It was difficult to leave the building, placing my students in the hands of a less than qualified individual. This half-day concept only lasted a couple of days before the administration shut us out. Each morning all the teachers would gather outside of the middle school where the board office was also located. The doors were locked and the school board's hired guards, affectionately called "The Green Garbage" because of their uniforms, would protect the school from teacher intrusion. They were also there to protect "substitute teachers," not so affectionately called "scabs," who were being brought in past us. Of course the press was there, newspapers and television. It's big news when a school is shut down because of a teacher strike.

The inevitable altercations arose between teachers, guards, and the substitutes. In all the confusion one male teacher's knee accidentally and repeatedly struck a guard's groin. Other teachers, intending to protect this teacher, quickly removed him from school property. All of this was caught on video tape, but later in court, the tape was inconclusive and the teacher could not be charged with battery. This is but one incident of the degenerating attitude and even violent behavior on the part of all participants.

Please remember that we are talking about teachers. People, like myself, who went to college to learn how to teach children. People, who probably could have earned more money in another profession but had a heart to work with children.

While the guards blocked the entrance to the middle school, teachers blocked the parking entrance to substitutes. Worse, the teachers let some of the substitutes bring their cars onto the property so they could surround and terrorize these people. It is interesting to reflect on the individuals who rocked cars and spit all over the windows. Some were consummate professionals who a few weeks earlier were appalled by the very use of the word, "scab." Now they spat on other individuals, shook their fists in their faces, and screamed with incredible vehemence, "SCAB." Needless to say, many of these guest instructors never returned.

A court order forced the teachers to either go back to work or be on strike the entire day. We were also forbidden to be on school property. From that day on, and for the next several weeks, each union member was assigned to a post. Elderly teachers and union leaders had the enviable task of manning telephones and taking coffee out to the picketers. Even though I worked at the middle school, I, along with a couple of other male teachers, was assigned to picket at one of the district's elementary buildings. It happened to be the most visible building in the district. The union felt the need to send a few male teachers to protect the female elementary teachers who had taught in that building. I will guarantee you that most female elementary teachers need absolutely no protection from anybody on the face of the earth. In reality, they are as fearsome a lot as can be found anywhere. At times I watched them become positively vicious as they attacked vans with substitute teachers and verbally abused the guards. One even spat on a substitute teacher's head when they were in the county courthouse for a hearing.

Day after day we watched most of our students go into the school buildings. Day after day we watched inadequate adults pretend to teach them. We heard rumors about many of the students wreaking havoc in the classrooms. Many teachers delighted in the news. Day after day we would meet for breakfast, absorb the sneers of the general public, make jokes that became less humorous over time, and go to designated posts.

The administration did not buckle and the public's nominal support quickly waned. Administrators kept getting their paychecks and so did state labor leaders. Our particular state leader, who had early on advised us that at all times we were to abide by the law, turned to page two of his "How to Go on Strike" manual. Sleaze's latest brilliancy involved picketing board members' homes on a Saturday morning. Give the guy credit; he was trying to do something to earn his big paycheck. Of course he wouldn't be out there on the line. He was the mastermind. Besides that, I think he had a family reunion that day with some great white sharks.

I only lasted about five minutes in front of the board member's home to which I was assigned. I respected the lady and when she came to the window and waved, I waved back and went home. I was one of the lucky ones. At another board member's home, a family member drove past the teachers with a fully loaded manure spreader. After passing the teachers, the spreader was no longer fully loaded. If nothing else, it was a statement of my feelings about this whole strike business.

By the sixth week I had had it. I was walking the picket line in the rain with my head down. I really didn't care to be recognized. It was raining, a very cold January rain, and I was coming down with bronchitis. The horn of a vehicle caught my attention. People often would drive by and honk. When we would look up we would either get a thumbs-up or another digit up. This time it was not a thumb I was looking at. Two construction workers in a pickup truck with out-of-state plates had just informed me that they were somewhat unhappy with my life choices. That was IT.

In a fit of anger I rushed across the street, jumped into my car, and started after them. No one ever accused me of being the brightest bulb in the chandelier. I finally caught up with these two fellows at the local McDonald's. They were in the drive-thru line placing an order. I honked my horn. They looked up. No, I did not express myself in digital diplomacy, but I did have a point to make.

"I really don't appreciate jerks driving past me and flashing their IQ score in my direction."

"Huh?"

Point proven. "I said I don't like jerks flashing their IQ scores in my direction."

"Yea?" It was the snappy comeback I expected.

I drove off and headed on down the road to get gas for my car at the local service station, never expecting to see them again. I was wrong. As I am ready to pull out of the gas station they were pulling in with the intention of furthering our discussion. Any sensible person would have just driven on down the road and hoped that they would go away. But after six weeks on a picket line, who is sensible? I drove over to their truck to elaborate on my concern as to their ethics and intelligence.

After a short conversation in which my parentage was brought into question, I discovered that one of the men had a niece in the school who was upset over the strike. I shared my feelings about the strike and how frustrating our situation had become as teachers. Fortunately, one of these construction workers was a reasonable man who actually apologized for what they had done. The driver, on the other hand, made the point as they were leaving that his friends called him one bad ** %$#^&. I didn't tell him that my friends called me "sensei." I was very blessed that I did not end up in traction by the end of the day.

When the strike finally ended, all of the teachers had lost a considerable amount of money that they would never recover. More significantly, the students were never the same. It was strange returning to my classroom.

The walls and windows were covered with decorated construction paper Easter eggs, hundreds of them. So much for education. I was happy that my students still treated me with respect. Many teachers never did regain that respect in their classes.

Additionally, those principals who had worked closely with their faculty in the best interests of children never reestablished that bond with their fellow educators. Old Snake Tongue lasted one more year in the district and ended up with serious health problems. Sleaze went on to help other schools along the road to bargaining bliss. The community never really forgave us for a variety of reasons. And teachers who had walked side by side on the picket line began to resent and blame one another. The school district, to this day, has not truly recovered and perhaps never will.

As I reflect on that strike, I am amazed at how well-intended people can lose their perspective, their purpose for existence. In the case of the school, administrators and teachers alike became so obsessed with winning that they all lost. Of greater significance is the fact that the children lost. They lost valuable time in instruction. They also lost respect for their teachers and principals. It did not matter to them who was right and who was wrong. What did matter was the sense that they were cheated out of something valuable.

During and after the strike, I also saw an unwillingness of people and groups of people to compromise.

There are times when compromise is not a good idea. To compromise the truth is to deny that truth. To compromise your principles is to deny yourself. But how many times do individuals and groups fail to compromise in the realm of opinion? How many times does our own personal agenda stand in the way of the greater good?

Fortunately, churches do not go on strike. Unfortunately, church members too often go to war with each other. They will frequently choose sides based on an offense or perceived offense and work diligently to ensure victory for their side. When such a scenario happens in the church, as with school strikes, everyone loses. Perhaps the greatest losers are those individuals who are new in the faith or are struggling with their own spiritual maturation. It is at the expense of all members of the Body that such wars take place. It is at the expense of our ability to lead others to Christ that we fight wars of opinion and preference.

We must honestly ask ourselves when we are facing conflict, "Is this issue really that important? Is it worth the battle? Am I willing to pay the price to get my own way?" And most of all, we must ask, "Is it worth making others pay a price for our personal vindication?"

Paul says, "Do nothing out of selfish ambition or vain conceit, but in humility consider others better than yourselves" (Philippians 2:3).

Joy Stealers

*I*t was the second day after back surgery. I was resting, if that is possible, in a hospital bed after practicing getting up and down for the doctor's benefit. I wanted to go home and was willing to endure the back spasms to fool the doctor just to get out of there. I had been very ill as a result of the anesthetic and had other complications. My face was a light gray color. Regardless, I was making progress and the surgeon assured me that all was well and I would recover completely. The nursing staff complimented me on my positive attitude. They were easier to fool than the doctor. Deep inside I was a whimpering pup. But, I was on the road to recovery and I was happy.

That is, until some of my "friends" paid me a visit. That their mouths dropped open when they first came into the room should have been an indicator as to what was coming.

"You look terrible!" This was from a woman who had to sneak up on a mirror. Besides that, what could you expect? I was wearing an outfit that did nothing to cover my derrière, I hadn't been able to wash my hair, what there was of it, for three days, I needed a shave, and food that I had tried to eat did not remain were it belonged. Nevertheless, I was still happy. I was going home soon and all was good, very good.

"I knew a man, a friend of mine, who had back surgery. He looked like you do right after his surgery. Six months after he was released from the hospital he died of a cancer that was in his back."

Her next words should have been, "Shall we pray?"

Did I mention that I wasn't feeling so well? The morose covered me like a blanket.

You've been there. You buy a new car. You are anxious for your friends and family to see it. You did all of your research, checked your budget, made your deal, arranged your financing, and drove it off the lot. Parking places are at least two blocks away from any other vehicle. And every time you park it and walk away, you glance back to make sure it's still there. No speck of dust is permitted to reside on its shiny shell. And absolutely no eating in the car. What a joy this automotive delight has brought you!

That is, until you show it to your father-in-law.

"See you bought a Hupmobile. I bought a Hupmobile once. Worst car I ever had. Spent more time in the shop then it did on the road. Piece of junk!"

No sense parking four miles from the store. And, what's a little dust? By the way, does anyone want to stop at Burger Bill's on the way home for a sandwich for the road?

"Who are you getting to build your new house?"

"Better Build. I have heard nothing but good reports on them. Top quality at a reasonable price."

"I don't know who you've been talking to but my cousin had Better Build construct his home. It's a wonder the place is still standing. He's looking for someone to unload that money pit on."

The list goes on. A new job. A future son-in-law. Even when you volunteer to do something for the church family. Someone is always there to be a naysayer, a joy stealer. Your anticipation is great, your joy is bursting within you, and you are on top of the world when the balloon popper shows up to bring you back to your mundane reality.

During one snowy December day as I was traveling into town, I saw an older lady shoveling snow from her driveway. With joy I pulled my car to the side of the road, took the shovel from her frail and chilled hands, and shoveled that driveway for her. As soon as I finished and with as big a smile as I could muster I uttered the fateful words, "Merry Christmas."

Did she offer me a cup of coffee or a hot chocolate? Did she say, "Thank you"? Did she even return the traditional Christmas greeting? No. None of the above. With a scowl she simply replied, "We don't celebrate Christmas." POP!

I wanted to say, "Bah, humbug" and shovel all of the snow back into that driveway. But I didn't. I just took my deflated and tired self back to my car and back to my business.

Perhaps the worst joy stealers were those religious leaders who confronted Jesus and His disciples on a regular basis. On one occasion Jesus saw a man in Jerusalem, probably at the temple gates and begging for alms, who had been born blind (see John 9). This was a man who had never seen the light of day, never had seen a sunset, a building or animal, the spring flowers on the Judean hillside, or even his mother's face.

After answering the disciples' questions concerning accountability for this man's blindness, Jesus mixed His spit with dirt to make a poultice. He placed that paste on the man's eyes and sent him to the Pool of Siloam to wash the mud from his eyes. Can you imagine the man's anticipation as he made that journey? Maybe he received help from a sympathetic bystander. Maybe he journeyed alone and felt his way along familiar buildings. Can you imagine the man's anticipation as he knelt in front of that pool and tentatively sunk his hands into the water? Can you imagine his anticipation as he brought that water to his face and began to wash the poultice from his eyes?

And can you imagine the joy he experienced as he saw for the first time? Was it is own hands that he saw first? Did he stare at them momentarily or did he immediately begin to gaze about and take in all of the sites that surrounded him.

"That's a donkey! Has to be a donkey. I can tell by that terrible noise it's making. They are funnier to look at than they sound. Oops! Excuse me mister. I didn't see you for a second! Look at that. No doubt, a tree. And that sun. Wow!"

Full of joy this man heads for home. At first, some of his neighbors denied the possibility. This may look like that blind guy but it can't be so.

"No. It's me. I'm the man."

"And how is it that you see?"

The man reviewed his experience with Jesus in an unadorned narrative probably thinking that they would be as excited as he. Their reply, "Where is this man?" Shortly thereafter this joyous man was brought before the religious leaders of his day. These were men who had power: power to isolate him from the entire Jewish community, power to alienate him from his family and friends.

Instead of rejoicing that a man who was born blind could now see, they were concerned about specific legal questions. The "problem" was two-fold. First of all, the healing was done on the Sabbath and with the use of mud. And secondly, the healing was seemingly done by this one called Jesus. In the investigation, the man reiterated his story of how he received his sight. Although his interrogators were threatening and belligerent, he could not be shaken from his account. The only fact that held weight was that he could now see and Jesus was responsible.

Unable to break through the man's defense, they called in his parents. You would expect Mom and Dad to be overjoyed by the miracle that brought sight to their son. But their joy was stolen by their fear of a group of self-righteous and abusive religious leaders.

"Is this your son?"

"Yes."

"How is it that he can now see? Who opened his eyes?"

"Don't know. Ask him. He is of age."

Before we are too critical of Mom and Dad maybe we should take a look inside ourselves. Would we have been any bolder given the circumstances? Are we any bolder in the cause of truth in any circumstance?

These religious leaders, these Pharisees with their well-polished phylacteries, called the man back in with the intention of breaking him down.

"Give God the glory!" He was giving God the glory but this was their attempt to make him confess to some collusion between him and Jesus.

"We know this man [Jesus] is a sinner."

"Can't speak to this sinner issue, but I'll tell you boys one thing I know, and you cannot and you will not dissuade me from this one thing. I was blind but now I see. Argue with that."

"What did He do to you? How did He open your eyes?" I think I've done business with this lawyer.

"I have already told you and you did not listen. Why

do you want to hear it again? Do you want to become His disciples too?" I really like this guy. No formal education. No fancy social position. No prestigious job. He was a man at the bottom of the social ladder in his day, but he would not be shaken from the truth. He would not permit these self-important, arrogant men to steal his joy.

His boldness, and the truth upon which he built this boldness, caused his accusers to revert to name calling and then the final accusation. "You are this man's [Jesus's] disciple. We are disciples of Moses. We don't even know where He [Jesus] comes from."

The man's final volley was the coup de grace and one that got him thrown out. "Now that is remarkable! You don't know where He comes from, yet He opened my eyes. He could not have opened my eyes if He were not from God."

Jesus met the man after he was thrown out by the Pharisees and gave him even greater sight and greater joy when He shared with him the spiritual sight that comes from knowing the Master.

The threats, accusations, haughty spirit, and conde-scending attitude of the Pharisees could not shake this man from the joy he had received from Jesus. Regardless of what they did to him he was better off than he was before he met the Lord.

And so are we.

We can have joy during the good times because we

know He cares for us and every blessing that we have comes from Him. We know that when we seek first His kingdom and His righteousness we have no need to worry because He provides for us (see Matthew 6:33).

We can have joy during the difficult times because "we know that in all things God works for the good of those that love Him" (Romans 8:28). We know that no hardship can separate us from the love of God and that we are "more than conquerors through Him who loved us" (Romans 8:37).

Don't be a joy stealer. "Rejoice with those who rejoice" (Romans 12:15).

Don't permit others to steal your joy.

"May the God of hope fill you with all joy and peace as you trust in Him, so that you may overflow with hope by the power of the Holy Spirit" (Romans 15:13).

Hidden Behind the Screen

A stuffed Buckeye Brutus sat on the back of the couch. Special treats were at hand. Except for emergencies, no telephone calls were to be made to our house, no visitors were to knock upon our door. Dee was in her special chair and I in mine. The game was scheduled for 3:30 and we were ready. Dinner that night would not take place until after the final gun. The television set was on and set for viewing and recording. We just love the DVR. Every disputed play can be reviewed at our convenience. Every great play can be enjoyed again and again. Our nerves were taut and we knew we would be exhausted when it was all over.

A major network, national coverage, and about one million cameras to catch every angle of the action were all there to guarantee a walk through football heaven. Then, the announcement of the announcers. Nooooooo. Not Has Been and Never Was. We had seen these two guys announce other games, if you could call it announcing a game. They both suffer from an extreme case of distraction and distract the audience with their malady. Perhaps this time it would be different. Surely they realize that this is the number one rated Ohio State Buckeyes playing a top contender with national championship implications on the line. Surely they will not be so self-absorbed that they forget about the game. Surely they will not have so many asides to the action that they and the audience miss much of the game.

Have you ever noticed that when you talk to someone on the television set, they don't respond? They can't seem to hear a word you are saying, even if you raise your voice to a bellow. Dee and I survived missing plays because they were doing color commentary on past players, the coaches' wives, and a multitude of other unimportant trivia. It was only when they spent ten minutes talking about how they had gone bowling the night before that I lost it. It was bad enough listening to Never Was and Has Been, but to add to our frustration, the camera was on them the entire time.

I yelled loud enough to be heard three counties away, "THE GAME. GET YOUR HEAD IN THE GAME. PUT THE CAMERA ON THE GAME. SHUT UP (Yes, I said that in the heat of battle.) I DON'T CARE ABOUT YOUR BOWLING."

"IT'S ABOUT THE GAME!!!!!!"

My outburst did no good whatsoever. They continued to be absorbed in themselves and other insignificant subjects. By the way, the Buckeyes did win, much to the dismay of Never Was and Has Been.

Football games are not the only time people major in minors, and this at the expense of what is really important. While we were doing research for a new book, Dee and I visited various congregations to get an idea of what their programs and members were like. We learned much more than the congregations or their leadership would have ever guessed, and perhaps, would have wanted us to learn. We usually went online to locate specific congregations and to learn in advance certain characteristics of that particular group.

One Sunday, after visiting their web site, we chose to attend a congregation in our brotherhood. All indications were that this group would be conservative and somewhat traditional. We put on our Sunday best, picked up our Bibles, and headed off to worship our God in spirit and in truth and to fellowship with the saints. When we arrived, the people were very friendly and the building was clean and modest. The Sunday bulletin raised our expectations and all looked very promising as we took our seats.

Suddenly a large screen was lowered to receive computer generated announcements, words to the songs, and sermon notes. The entertainers took their place on the stage. Little did we know that Jimi Hendrix and his back-up band would be leading the Showself Service. When the wannabe rockers hit those guitars and drums, we were positive we were at Woodstock. Trying to be objective, we ignored our forthcoming headaches. The words on the screen had little importance as the only ones singing were the Me Team and a handful of members who seemed to know the rockaJesus songs. Jimi's solo before the morning message was something never to be forgotten. I'm sure there were actual words but we have no idea what they were.

Still, we had hope. The speaker, a.k.a. preacher, took his place behind the pulpit. He had prepared a unique message that I had only heard two other times. It was a message about geese. Throughout the message on the screen behind him flashed different pictures of geese along with pictures of Barney Fife from the *Andy Griffith Show* and other celebrities. After the message was an invitation song, although we were not sure as to what we were being invited to.

As we were leaving, Dee asked me if I saw the lighted cross. "What cross?" I asked.

"The cross behind the screen." No, I hadn't seen the cross. Unfortunately, I doubt if anyone did.

Dee and I do not have a problem when guitars and drums are used in the assembly. Please ensure, though, that all things are done "in a fitting and orderly way" (I Corinthians 14:40). Please ensure that the music is not so loud that it distracts from congregational singing. As far as I'm concerned, feel free to use geese to illustrate a scriptural point. Just make sure there is a scriptural point.

There is, however, a bigger problem than musical instruments and shallow sermons. It's the problem of focus. Through our research, Dee and I have found that many of the congregations we visited were absorbed in themselves and their marketing strategies. Unfortunately this direction has been taken at the expense of the message of the cross.

I do not wish to be judgmental or harsh. I just wish to ask, "Have we, the church, lost sight of who we are supposed to be?" I am not questioning the intentions of many well-meaning church leaders and members who have decided to take up the banner of a "more relevant" Christianity. Please remember, though, that the very best intentions often have deplorable outcomes. I am not questioning the intentions of those in evangelical circles who have taken up this banner. I am, however, questioning the wisdom of such direction. Paul said, "… but we preach Christ crucified: a stumbling block to Jews and foolishness to Gentiles, but to those whom God has called, both Jews and Greeks, Christ the power of God and the wisdom of God. For the foolishness of God is wiser than man's wisdom, and the weakness of God is stronger than man's strength" (I Corinthians 1:23–25).

Have we, the church, hidden the cross of Christ behind a screen of slick marketing and sophisticated advertisement? In our attempt to become more relevant to "grow the church," have we become irrelevant as the light of the world and the salt of the earth (see Matthew 5:13–16)?

I am aware of congregations which have surveyed the community to determine the kind of church they would like to see in the neighborhood, and these churches adjusted their programs accordingly. I thought the Lord Jesus already determined what the church should be and what its purpose was when He said, "On this rock, I will build my church" (Matthew 16:18). I thought He made it quite clear when He said, "All authority in heaven and on earth has been given to Me. Therefore go and make disciples of all nations, baptizing them in the name of the Father and of the Son and of the Holy Spirit, and teaching them to obey everything I have commanded you. And surely I am with you always, to the very end of the age" (Matthew 28:18–20). He spoke clearly when He said, "Heaven and earth will pass away, but My words will never pass away" (Matthew 24:35). By what authority do any of us say we have a new and improved version of Christianity in the name of reaching the lost?

Have we, the church, hidden the cross behind a screen of entertainment? Call me old-fashioned, but when I see a young woman stand in front of a congregation to lead the song service behaving like Madonna or Britney Spears at one of their concerts, I have trouble relating it to singing praises to His name. The same is true of any individual, male or female, old or young. Is our purpose to entertain and be entertained? Is it to glorify or be glorified? If I stand before the multitudes and say that I am doing all for the glory of God and my actions say that I am doing so for self-glorification, which voice is heard? I like entertainment and am all for fun, but do we believe that it is the purpose of the church to make sure everyone is having fun? Or is it the purpose of the church to seek and save the lost and to glorify the Creator through His Son.

Have we, the church, hidden the cross behind a screen of shallow messages that fail to speak the truth, all of the truth, in love? How many of our preachers study or even know how to study the Word of God in this day and age? How many even care to? How many preachers are so afraid of offending someone that they themselves are offended by the message of the cross? God bless those Godly men who stand up before this generation and without compromise share the message of the cross that leads to salvation.

More so, have we lost sight of the One we represent, who we are suppose to honor and worship? We must know and accept that it's not about me. The assembly should give me strength through the study of His Word and the fellowship with His saints. But it is still not about me. The assembly does not exist to entertain me or make me feel good about myself. It's not about me. Even when I look into a mirror, I must reflect, "It is not about me!"

It's about Him and what He did for us on the cross. The apostle Paul said, "May I never boast except in the cross of our Lord Jesus Christ ..." (Galatians 6:14).

"IT'S ABOUT HIM AND WHAT HE DID FOR US ON THE CROSS OF CALVARY!"

I'm sure that I am not talking to a television set.

Hair Tonic and Real Estate Agents

No doubt about it. There it was. It wasn't very large
and its specific type was unknown. But nonetheless,
it was definitely there. Dee and I were both looking at
it and its existence was undeniable. Yep! It was a tree.
Anyone who has traveled through a small, eastern Ohio
town as Dee and I were on that day knows that the
appearance of a tree is hardly unusual. In any direction
these marvels of nature can be seen. But nevertheless,
we were so surprised that we pulled the car to the side of
the road so we could stare in wonder. This tree was not
unique because it existed. It was unique because it was
growing out of the chimney of a dilapidated two-story
house. The chimney looked as though it were ready to
fall through the roof at any moment.

After the initial shock, we began to visually examine
the rest of the property. The house, as I noted, was on
the verge of collapse. The yard was a tangle of weeds and
much neglected shrubbery. Then, a shock that exceeded
the surprise of seeing a tree growing from the chimney.
A sign in the front yard. A neat, clearly printed sign

indicating that this building, this house, this run-down structure housed the offices of a real estate agency.

Now I can't speak for you but this is not the place I would go if I were interested in purchasing property. First of all, I would be afraid to step onto the porch for fear of falling through the floor. More importantly, they really didn't represent the kind of property I would be interested in. Can you imagine the conversation?

"Well, Mr. Berresford, let us show you a fixer-upper." (The only thing that could fix up one of their fixer-uppers would be a match.)

Or perhaps, "Mr. Berresford, we have a real beauty for you that we are sure will fit your budget." (If this is their idea of beauty, I still need that match.)

I would no sooner buy real estate through that agency than I would buy a hair growth tonic from a hair folliclely challenged man. Nor would I take tax advice from someone who is always in trouble with the IRS. I also would not follow time management and organizational strategies from an individual whose life is so unorganized that they can't find themselves in a mirror.

Most people probably think the same way I do about these things. We expect a salesman, business owner, or consultant to effectively and positively represent their product, business, or advice by who they are as well as by what they say.

Should we expect any less of those who wear the name of Christ and profess to be His disciples? Should I expect any less of myself?

Many in the world are looking for a better life. They are looking for hope for themselves and their families. They want better. They want the peace which transcends all understanding (see Philippians 4:7). Often these individuals look to the church and those who call themselves Christians. What do they see?

My prayer is that they see those who "reflect the Lord's glory, [and] are being transformed into His likeness …" (II Corinthians 3:18). It is my prayer that they see ambassadors of Christ (see II Corinthians 5:20) representing the King in what they say and who they are. It is my prayer that they see individuals and congregations who have a passion for the truth and a compassion for people. It is my prayer that those who are weary and burdened (see Matthew 11:28) and all those who hunger and thirst for righteousness (see Matthew 5:6) will see godly characteristics in me.

But do they? The rap on the church and its members for generations has been the charge of hypocrisy. Often this accusation has simply been an excuse to avoid a commitment to Christ. But too often it has been too true. How many times has a non-believer witnessed professed Christians being guilty of what they claim to abhor in others? When the non-Christian looks in our direction do they see righteousness or self-righteousness; holiness or holier-than-thou-ness?

Subsequently, Dee and I drove past the house that had a tree in the chimney. The transformation was astonishing. Had we not seen it in its prior state, we would never have believed what the real estate agency could do with that building. They had taken this run-down place that looked ready for the demolition team and turned it into a show place. If I need property, I will not hesitate to pay them a visit.

Maybe its time for all of us to do a little personal transformation so we can better represent our King. We cannot do it on our own but if we yield our will to His, He will make us anew. Will we be perfect? No. Will we shine a brighter light and convey a clearer message? Absolutely.

Paul admonishes us in the book of Romans to "not conform any longer to the pattern of this world, but be transformed by the renewing of [our] mind" (Romans 12:2). The word "transformed" is translated from the word "metamorphoses." The English and the Greek indicate a complete change in the way someone or something looks or acts. It is the word that is used to describe the change of a caterpillar into a butterfly.

When I examine their appearance and characteristics, there is no doubt as to which one is the caterpillar and which one is the butterfly. Likewise there should be no doubt as to whether I have been transformed into His likeness and reflect His glory.

A Yellow Raincoat

When I was a young child my family was very poor. Part of the reason was the terrible economy. Of greater significance were my father's health problems, which were a direct and indirect result of what he experienced in Europe during WWII.

One of the first houses I remember living in was actually a shack. It was home and I really didn't know that most children were much better off materially than I. Water was gotten from a hand-pumped well. An old and dangerous kerosene stove, whose smell is still a vivid memory, heated the house. During the daytime, if one needed to use the facilities, they were located down a short path in back of the house. Cold weather made for an especially uncomfortable excursion. At nighttime, an old pot served the same purpose. Emptying that pot was always a terrible duty for man, woman, or child.

We never had a great variety in our diet but we were never hungry either. Supper usually consisted of navy beans and a ham bone, or hot dogs and baked beans, or a combination of green beans, a few potatoes, and a small touch of bacon fat for taste. I think there is a pattern here. We might also have homemade vegetable soup with upwards to three or four different vegetables in it and flavored with a beef bone. I could never get my own children to appreciate these delicacies.

Breakfast, however, was the best meal of the day. On school days, my mother would make oatmeal or Cream of Wheat and always hot chocolate. On special days, we would have cinnamon-sugar toast. It was a breakfast fit for a king. We would huddle around that old stove and enjoy a warmth that exceeded its ability.

When it was time to leave for school I headed down the hill to a church building where all the children in the area would wait for the school bus. The walk, from my five-year-old perspective, was about twenty miles. It was in reality about a quarter of a mile, but not uphill both ways in six feet of snow. For some reason I can vividly remember looking out of the window of that bus back up the hill to the old shack I lived in.

My mother was one of the greatest women I have ever known. She did more with what she had than most could imagine possible. Somehow she scraped together enough money to buy a yellow raincoat with a hood for me. You know the kind, the raincoat that was pictured in the children's books of the 1950s. She was proud that she was able to provide such a raincoat for her son and looked forward to the first rainy day so he could wear it to the bus stop. She could just see the little fellow march down to the church with his head held high.

Unfortunately, I was the little fellow and too often saw life differently than my mother.

The first rainy day came. The bright, shiny raincoat was taken off the hanger. The five-year-old boy was brought forth to don the new apparel. Mom was all smiles. I never saw a person so happy over a little rain.

"Let's put on your raincoat. Pourin' down rain and it'll keep you nice and dry."

"No." This was not a word my mother was accustomed to hearing come out of my mouth or a word that she received with grace.

She was surprisingly patient. "Come on. Let's hurry and get this coat on so you won't be late for the bus."

"No. I'm not wearing the raincoat."

Like I mentioned before, my mother was a great woman. One of the things that made her great was her ability to take on a challenge. She was more than up to the challenge of a stubborn five-year-old.

"Put the coat on, NOW!" As she was in the process of saying this, she was putting first my right arm and then my left arm into the sleeves. "And fasten it up." The little metal snaps were closing faster than she could say the words. "And the hood goes UP." And it did.

I take after my mother a good deal and this had become a true battle of wills. She may have been bigger and stronger, but I was five years old and a force to be reckoned with. "I'm NOT wearing this coat to the bus stop!" But I did.

In those days, parents believed that belts were to be used for two things. One was to hold pants up; the other was to alter the behavior of a child. All the way to the bus stop I was accompanied by repeated encouragement from a narrow strip of leather. I cried and my mother cried but I did wear the coat and I did get on the bus and I did go to school, and believe me, when I came home that afternoon I was wearing the coat even though it was not raining. I have often wondered what my mother was thinking about on her walk back to the house that day in the rain without a raincoat or umbrella for herself.

Looking back on that brief time in my life, I appreciate more than I could have then what I had. It was not the big ticket items that made life special. It was the warmth, the caring, and the security that I had through my family. Oatmeal, ham and beans, and cornbread are better enjoyed in the right company than lobster and steak in a lifeless reality.

In this day, I think most of us spend so much time thinking about what we don't have and what we might get that we lose sight of what has been given to us. It is only after the fact that we look back and appreciate what was. Trouble is, we can't go back in time to enjoy those things again.

The expression "carpe diem" was made popular by the movie *Dead Poets Society*. Seize the day is the admonition but not seize the day by the Epicurean standard of eating and drinking and making merry. Carpe diem. Enjoy the moments that you have been given. Seize the day so when you look back you will remember how you drank in every wonderful opportunity and blessing God has given you. Carpe diem. Take time to appreciate the simplest things because most often they are the greatest things we will ever have or experience.

When I think about the infamous day of the yellow raincoat, I think more about the pain I must have caused my mother than the pain I suffered from the punishment she gave me. I think about her walk back to the house in the rain. I think of how my ingratitude hurt her.

How many times has my heavenly Father blessed me? Every good and perfect gift that I have comes from Him (see James 1:17). He provides for me in abundance. Not only does He provide for the things of this world, He gives me hope of eternal blessings through His son. Am I as ungrateful of His blessings as I was of my mother's gift those years ago?

I called my mother and thanked her for that yellow raincoat. I think I will also talk to my heavenly Father and thank Him for all that He has done for me.

Dunmovin

Dee thought moving four times in two years was a bit excessive. It wasn't because we were running from the rent collector. A change in jobs, moving to a bigger house to rent, and building a new home were the justifiable reasons for this exhausting endeavor. Once we were in our new place, Dee said that the only way to get her out of there would be in a pine box, not that she felt strongly about it.

Moving is tough business. Not only is there the taxing manual labor of boxing and unboxing your worldly possessions and hauling all of your furniture from one building to another, you have the added fun of dealing with utility companies. If you are moving to a new community, there is the additional stress of trying to locate all of those businesses, including doctors and dentists, you took for granted at your previous home. A long distance move may even cost you your support base, as you have become isolated from your previous church family, relatives, and friends. Finding a new church to attend is always difficult.

I'm sure that journeying from one place to another has always been complicated. No doubt the Pilgrims were apprehensive traveling across the Atlantic and planting roots in a new world. The pioneers during the westward expansion in this country suffered innumerable hardships in order to find a new home with new opportunities. Many had what has been called "wanderlust." They never felt at home, never believed that they had reached their final destination.

The Biblical Abraham understood the feeling of never truly being at home. So did his son and grandson, Isaac and Jacob. Even though God had given them a promised land, they felt as though they were strangers in a foreign country. They looked forward to something better, a city with foundations whose architect and builder is God. They had a form of wanderlust in that they admitted that they were aliens and strangers on the earth (see Hebrews 11:8–13).

The Apostle Paul expresses similar feelings when he says that for him to live was Christ-like but to die would be gain (see Philippians 1:21). He also talks about that day when death is swallowed up in victory and mortality is clothed with immortality (see I Corinthians 15:54). Although he was a Roman citizen, he counted his real citizenship to be in heaven (see Philippians 3:20–21).

Godly men and women have always understood the idea that they were pilgrims on this earth and that they could look forward to something much better when they went home to be with the Lord.

Our life on this earth is a journey. When we are young we tend to think that the journey here will last forever. We have an unrealistic sense of immortality and our view is often skewed by our age. We are "the kid," grandchild, son, daughter. We are youth. We are spring. If we fall down, we bounce back up and our pain is quickly forgotten. If we are wise we will look to an old timer for advice. Generally, we doubt the sagaciousness of that advice. As youth, we often scoff at the manner of those who have been granted years, little realizing how brief those years really are. We lack patience as we hurry to the next phase of our lives. Too often we wish away our lives always wanting to be older, believing that age brings freedom.

As young adults we find ourselves caught up in becoming and being parents and establishing our careers. We are so busy becoming that we sometimes forget to be. And we begin to accumulate more things. Things we think we want. Things we think we need.

As middle-aged adults we become the between generation, taking care of parents and children. Our jobs and the busyness of our days can rob us of the simple joys of appreciating both parents and children. We try to go to the gym for a workout but for some of us, it's just too much work. We look in the mirror trying to see our youth but see Dad or Mom instead. And we accumulate more things. We look forward to retirement so we can finally enjoy life.

But now … I am the old timer. I tend to spend more time looking back than looking forward. When I fall down, which seems to be more often, my pain does not quickly go away. I sometimes feel like Samson must have when Delilah said for the third time, "The Philistines are upon you" (Judges 16:20). When he rose to meet them, his strength was gone. For Samson, it was his disobedience to God that caused his weakness. It is not the Philistines, though, that bind me. It is Father Time. He always seems to win.

Youth now tell me, "Step aside, old fellow. We have places to go and things to do." And I smile even as others smiled at me when I was young. I remember as a small child visiting a neighbor friend of mine. His father was sitting in a chair resting. I asked him, "How can you just sit there and not do anything?" He smiled and simply replied, "Someday you'll know." And I do.

And we wonder what we are going to do with all of the things we accumulated and have no use for any longer.

At times it seems so long ago but spring was just yesterday, the summer passed quickly, fall is here, and winter—winter is just around the corner.

Yes, our life is a journey; a very brief journey even if we are granted many years upon this earth. If it is lived for the glory of Christ, it will be a journey of joy looking forward to a destination of joy. There will be pitfalls and difficulties. There will be pain and suffering. Remember, moving is an exhausting endeavor, but we can follow the example of our Lord "who for the joy set before Him endured the cross, scorning its shame, and [who] sat down at the right hand of the throne of God" (Hebrews 12:2).

Recently Dee and I were traveling to a speaking engagement when we passed a large, beautiful brick home. The sign in the front yard confirmed our suspicions that this was a funeral home. It clearly read, "Dunmovin." How ironically appropriate! We later found out that this was not a funeral home but a gift shop. How ironically appropriate!

In Christ, the day is coming when we will be done moving and we will enter into the gift of everlasting life, experiencing the joy and riches of His heavenly kingdom. Dee wants two words placed on her headstone, "Gone Home." How appropriate!

DAVID BERRESFORD is a minister and a retired school principal. With a Bachelor of Science degree in history and religion and a Master of Educational Administration degree, David draws from his extensive educational and real-life experiences for *A Yellow Raincoat and Other Memories*, his first published book of stories.

When he's not writing or chopping wood at his home in Wooster, Ohio, David can be found traveling with his wife Darlene, visiting with their five children, rough-housing with their grandchildren, or refereeing his black lab Alex and his cat Sooty. Visit David at his website *www.A Journey To Hope . net*.